KENWOOD

C000258796

THE
COMPLETE COOKERY BOOK
FOR THE
CHEF & MAJOR

Sophie Buchmann

THE
COMPLETE COOKERY BOOK
FOR THE
CHEF & MAJOR

Published by Kenwood Limited,
New Lane, Havant, Hampshire PO9 2NH

First Published 1995
© Kenwood Limited 1995

ISBN 0-9526262-0-9

Recipe Development	Sophie Buchmann
Photography	Whitelight
Food Styling	Sunil Vijayakar

Designed and printed in Great Britain by
Print 4 Limited, a Kenwood company

CONTENTS

THE FOOD MIXER

THE TOTAL FOOD PREPARATION CENTRE

ACKNOWLEDGMENTS

The person whose name is on the front of the book can rarely take all the credit and this book is definitely not an exception. Acknowledgement must go to the team whose combined effort has made this book possible:-

Penny Hurley, who first initiated the project, and has seen it through from its conception to the long task of editing the copy and finally the publication.

Lloyd Allen and Darren Spinks, who have put their own artistic skills into the design and layout.

Brian Timmons and Alan Turner from Whitelight, need I say more – the photos speak for themselves.

Sunil Vijayakar, whose imagination captured the images we all had in mind for the photographs, allowing him to choose the correct props, styling them together brilliantly.

Liz Eacott and Anne-Marie Toman, for their superb illustrations.

Roy Dillon, who has overseen all the work carried out by Print 4.

Karen Boughton, who typed and assisted Penny during the first stages of the book and Julie Long, for typesetting and corrections in the final stages.

The overseas distributors and subsidiaries of Kenwood who lent advice and information and contributed some of their authentic recipes for the collection.

Kenwood colleagues for their help with the proof reading.

And last but not least, Daisy Nixon, who carefully tested each and every recipe in this book.

FOREWORD

COOKING AT HOME

Everyone imagines how their own kitchen should be. An old room with a flagstone floor and a vast second-hand pine table which has seen countless dishes placed on its surface; to one side, a wrought iron cooking range which needs constant nurturing if it is to bake the day's bread, and above it a shelf, craning under the weight of copper pans whose orange lustre has mellowed with use. Or it could be a new age kitchen, designed for the ultimate desire of any chef or cook; units in hard-wearing complex materials such as deep grey metals, fitted perfectly to make the most of space, stainless steel pans hanging from great ironwork hooks, ready for use on an ultra ceramic hob.

Whatever the style of kitchen, links with both old and new come through to create a warm place, full with rich aromas - from yeasty bread dough to onions slowly caramelising, or a basket of fresh, soft fruit gently warming by the window in the afternoon sun - ripe, sweet and ready to eat.

A kitchen is a bustling place which changes with the seasons: the early excitement of Spring when the sharp green young shoots produce vegetables so tender and new; Summer, which oozes richness into every dish and produces a glut of fruits so perfect for home-made preserves; Autumn leading to Winter, when the cook needs to be most resourceful. Whether stormy, sodden or frosted with the stars, the Winter night's air brings everyone to the warmth of the kitchen, where a large tureen of piping hot soup will rekindle the spirit and drive away the cold.

It is in the kitchen that your ingenuity reigns. Here is the place for artful plotting and planning. A sharpened appetite which comes from eating fresh, home-made and unadulterated food will encourage you to experiment more. It will demand more variety and in doing so lead to a greater appreciation for a varied diet.

The preparation of food has always been an inventor's paradise, and although not all ideas have lived through the test of time, anything that man has designed must be seen as a contribution to social progress and an aid to the creative cook.

The Kenwood Chef is certainly a creative cook's dream. With attachments for every function you can imagine how the Chef offers you a great adventure into the world of cookery. It allows your culinary imagination to run wild, providing you with an opportunity to prepare many exciting dishes which would otherwise seldom reach the dining table.

How to Use this Book

'The Complete Cookery Book for the Chef & Major' is almost a cookery course in its own right. If you started at the beginning, preparing and cooking your way through, by the end of the book you would have covered the majority of today's international cooking techniques. From making simple cakes to creating luxurious cream concoctions, baking German rye bread to making Italian style pasta, stir-frying the Chinese way to simply learning the ancient history of coffee: it's all in here.

Cooking can be fun. The secret is to choose a recipe that you really fancy eating and which doesn't require more time than you have to make it. Throughout this book I have taken preparation time into consideration and have, wherever possible, made methods simple and quick. There are some exceptions, so read through the recipe before you begin, to judge for yourself when you will have time enough to prepare it. Also whilst you are making a recipe, check whether it is suitable for freezing - you'll find it just as easy, and not much longer, to make several batches and freeze them for another day.

The recipes are set out in a slightly different way to a conventional book, arranged under the beater or attachment which is used in their preparation. Each beater and attachment has its own special chapter with recipes, an introduction and basic hints and tips to help you get the most from its use. Extra information such as model numbers can be found in A Guide to the Attachments on page 12. If you wish to select recipes for meals however, then the Menu Guide on page 160/161 lists all the recipes under their relevant course categories.

As all the recipes are for international use, I have endeavoured to use as many basic ingredients as possible - but even the same ingredients are often known by different names elsewhere. The Glossary on pages 152-159 will help with an explanation of what the ingredient is, its various different names and, where possible, an alternative item which can be used as a substitute. The Glossary also contains explanations of cooking terms which might not be so well known in all countries.

Finally my advice is, make space for the Kenwood Chef on your work surface and leave it there. This is one machine which should definitely not be left in the cupboard!

N.B. All the recipes in this book apply to both the Chef and the Major. For ease and space, where the Kitchen Machines are mentioned I shall refer to them collectively as the Chef.

INTRODUCTION

THE STORY OF THE *Kenwood* CHEF - SINCE 1947

It is now over 45 years since the 'Kitchen Revolution' took place – and what an impact it made too. Homes were transformed almost overnight as housewives laid down their sharp knives, hand whisks and wooden spoons, refusing to toil any longer. At last it was here - the Kenwood Chef had arrived.

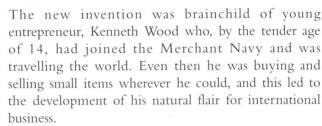

The new invention was brainchild of young entrepreneur, Kenneth Wood who, by the tender age of 14, had joined the Merchant Navy and was travelling the world. Even then he was buying and selling small items wherever he could, and this led to the development of his natural flair for international business.

In 1947 Mr Wood founded his first company, trading under the name of Kenwood Manufacturing Company Ltd., based in Woking, Surrey. Once in the business of electrical appliances, Kenneth's personal mission was to manufacture and sell products which would start out as luxury items and develop into a long-term necessity.

His first product was a toaster, followed closely by a twin beater mixer. The mixer sold well, but increasing competition, particularly from America, meant that in order to succeed, Kenneth Wood had to find something new. With his team of design engineers, he returned to the drawing board and set about re-designing the mixer.

The fruits of his labour were finally harvested in March 1950, when the revolutionary new machine was first launched at the famous Ideal Home Exhibition in London. With the facility for so many functions, it could no longer be called a mixer and was re-named the Kenwood Electric Chef A700. It sold for the princely sum of £19 10s.10d.

Before long, cargoes of product were being shipped all around the world, to Western Europe, South America, Canada and the USA. The Chef was fast gaining as high a reputation overseas as it was enjoying in its native Britain. The legend had begun......

Today the Kenwood Chef is an integral part of the kitchen, handed down from generation to generation, from parents to children.

Its reputation is as far-reaching as its functions. Known in over a hundred countries of the world, it is used both in the home and the commercial environment, by men and women alike.

The appeal of the Chef ranges wide - from busy parents with large families seeking reliability, to socialites, young and old, with a passion for dinner parties and a need for perfection. From weekday business people alias weekend hobby cooks desiring something different, to professional chefs who require all-round performance. Whatever or wherever the purpose, the Chef will always oblige.

Continuous study and development of the Chef throughout its long life has resulted in an appliance which today reigns supreme. From one basic model has grown an entire range of machines, each with different attributes to cater for today's more discerning users.

Powered by an advanced and efficient electronic motor the Chef will tackle any task it is given, handling delicate egg whites with gentle care whilst utilising its full strength to knead heavy bread doughs.

Known primarily for its major function as a traditional Food Mixer, the Chef contains a deep secret within its construction. For there are three extra concealed outlets located on the top and the front of the body, which operate a range of additional attachments, thereby converting the Kitchen Machine into a Total Food Preparation Centre.

Kenwood now has two sizes of Kitchen Machine - the original Chef, and the Major with a taller body, more powerful motor and a larger bowl. Used by semi-professionals as well as larger households, the Major caters more easily for greater quantities of basic preparations.

Two choices of colour are offered for both sizes of machine - traditional white and the professional silver finish. Underneath of course, all machine bodies are made from the same strengthened die-cast metal, whatever the colour on their surface.

Variations of top covers, head lifting buttons and levers, pulse features and speed controls all combine to distinguish each model in what has become the most impressive range of Kitchen Machines ever available.

THE BASIC TOOLS

PLANETARY ACTION

Just as the earth spins on its axis whilst circling around the sun, so the beaters of the Chef rotate whilst travelling around the inside of the bowl. The name given to this is Planetary Action.

This movement means that the beater can reach the entire inner surface of the bowl, ensuring what is known as a 'double-thorough' mixing to make sure every last morsel is incorporated.

THE BEATERS

Every single mixing function is catered for by one of the 3 beaters supplied with the Chef or Major. Their obvious rôles are for mixing, kneading and whisking but if you look closely at the recipe pages, you'll discover a great many additional uses.

THE BOWLS

'Kenlyte' and Stainless Steel Bowls can be interchanged on any of the Chef or Major models in the range. Both have their benefits and Chef users have their own preferences.

The Stainless Steel Bowl however, does tend to give slightly better results when whisking egg whites and cream or making pastry, as it retains the coolness in the mixture to give faster-acting results.

A D-shaped version of the Kenlyte Bowl facilitates the pouring of runny mixtures.

ACCESSORIES

The Splashguard - a useful bowl lid which holds the ingredients in the bowl during mixing and keeps it clear of dust when not in use.

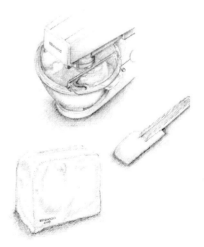

The Spatula - deemed by many Chef users to be the 'Best Ever Spatula' for its flexibility in scraping the very last crumbs from the bowl.

The Cover - hygienic and wipeable, the best way to keep your Chef clean and looking good.

NB: For details on using your Kenwood Chef or Major including maximum capacity tables, please consult the instruction booklet supplied with your Kitchen Machine.

The Attachments

Top Slow
Speed Outlet

Back High
Speed Outlet

Front Slow
Speed Outlet

Planet Hub

Variable Speed
Control

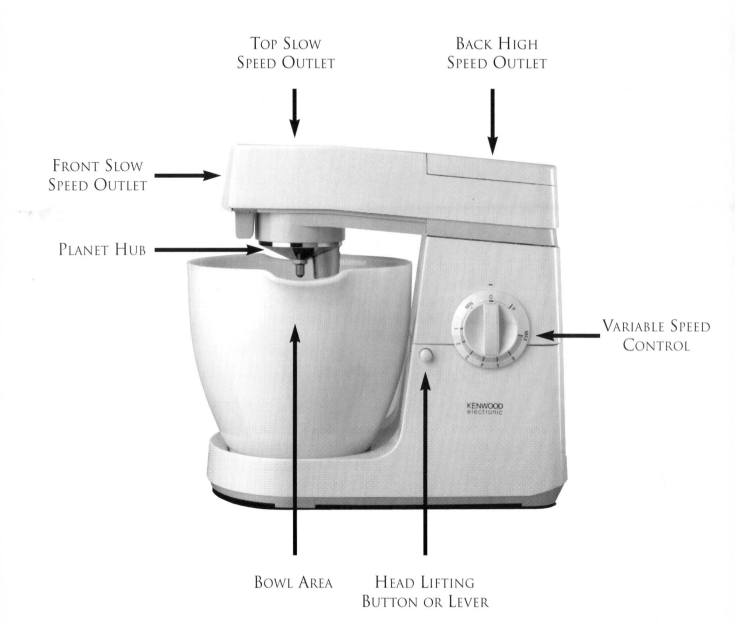

Bowl Area

Head Lifting
Button or Lever

Liquidiser

Mincer

Sausage Maker Adaptor

Kebbe Maker Adaptor

**High Speed
Slicer & Shredder**

**Slow Speed
Slicer & Shredder**

Juice Centrifuge

Citrus Juicer

Multi Mill

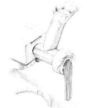

Pasta Extruder

Colander & Sieve

Potato Peeler

Grain Mill

Coffee Grinder

Cream Maker

Cookie Maker Adaptor

Fine Grater Adaptor

Bean & Peel Slicer

Can Opener

Ice Cream Maker

A GUIDE TO THE ATTACHMENTS

	Attachments	Part No.	Fits		Outlet Speed/Location				Recipe Pages
			Chef	Major	Slow/Bowl	Slow/Top	Slow/Front	High/Back	
Beaters	Balloon Whisk		Relevant size		✓				38 - 45
	Dough Hook		included with		✓				30 - 37
	K Beater		Chef or Major		✓				14 - 29
Attachments	Bean & Peel Slicer	A932	✓	✓			✓		136 - 139
	Can Opener	A978	✓	✓			✓		140 - 143
	Citrus Juicer	A995	✓	✓		✓			80 - 85
	Coffee Grinder	A979	✓	✓			✓		116 - 119
	Colander & Sieve	A992	✓	✗	✓				100 - 105
		A930	✗	✓	✓				
	Cookie Maker Adaptor	A925	fits A920 & A940				✓		124 - 129
	Cream Maker	A927	✓	✓			✓		120 - 123
	Fine Grater Adaptor	A924	fits A920 Only				✓		130 - 135
	Grain Mill	A941	✓	✓			✓		110 - 115
	High S. Slicer & Shredder	A929	✓	✓				✓	74 - 79
	Ice Cream Maker	A953	✓with Kenlyte Bowl		✓				144 - 149
		A954	with Kenlyte Bowl ✓		✓				
		A955	✓	✓	✓				
	Juice Centrifuge	A935	✓	✓				✓	80 - 87
	Kebbe Maker Adaptor	A937	fits A920				✓		72 - 73
		A943	fits A940				✓		
	Liquidiser Acrylic	A989/A993	✓	✓				✓	48 - 57
	Glass	A990/A994	✓	✓				✓	
	S. Steel	A996	✓	✓				✓	
	Mincer No. 7	A920	✓	✓			✓		58 - 65
	No. 8	A940	✓	✓			✓		
	Multi Mill	A938	✓	✓				✓	88 - 93
	Pasta Extruder	A936	✓	✓			✓		94 - 99
	Potato Peeler	A934	✓	✗	✓				106 - 109
		A952	✗	✓	✓				
	Sausage Maker Adaptor	A926	fits A920				✓		66 - 71
		A942	fits A940				✓		
	Slow S. Slicer & Shredder	A948	✓	✓			✓		74 - 79
Bowls	Kenlyte Bowl	19659	✓	✗	✓				
		26538	✗	✓	✓				
	Stainless Steel Bowl	18749	✓	✗	✓				
		18748	✗	✓	✓				
	D Shaped Bowl	28714	✓	✗	✓				
Accessories	Splashguard Round	31227	✓	✓					
	D Shaped	30238	✓	✗					
	Cover	29021	✓	✗					
		25639	✗	✓					
	Spatula	375948	✓	✓					

KENWOOD

Chef ❖ Major

The

Food Mixer

Cakes, Pastries... and a Whole Lot More

"Eating well gives a spectacular joy to life" Elsa Schiaparelli - *Shocking Life*

Many great cooks have showered their talents on creating a tea time feast - a table dressed with a linen cloth, abundant in scrumptious iced cakes oozing with cream fillings, and delectable, rich pastries.

However it is not always the elaborate sticky concoctions that draw people to the table - a 19th century Scottish farmer's wife attracted royals to tea with her plain, but perfect, scones! My mother, armed with her Kenwood Major and large farmhouse cooker, used to make trays of 'Goose Egg Sponge' which she kept in the freezer for unexpected visitors. Whatever the occasion and no matter how simple or lavish you want your baking to be, the K Beater will make it a success.

All manner of tasks from creaming butter and sugar for cakes to mashing potato, making biscuits into crumbs or gently stirring in flour and fruits - the K Beater does them all, its beautiful designed and angled fins sweeping their way around a deep, roomy bowl. It mixes to perfection, time after time, whether you are making a small batch of scones or a cake large enough to feed a hundred people.

It seems a shame that many people have discounted themselves as being poor pastry makers, believing the secret lies in a light, cool hand. The K Beater, being metal, definitely lends a cool touch and is also extremely gentle, producing excellent results every time. If you use the Stainless Steel Bowl you'll find it helps to keep the ingredients cool during mixing. Home-made pastry is always better than any shop-bought variety, so follow the recipes carefully and you too will have melt-in-the-mouth pies and tarts which will disappear before they are barely cool.

Hints & Tips

❖ Use the handles on the white bowl to pour the runny mixtures.

❖ Don't forget the Spatula for scraping the bowl clean.

❖ For cakes, best results are achieved when all the ingredients are at room temperature, unless the recipe specifies otherwise.

❖ Pastries prefer cooler ingredients, unless the recipe specifies otherwise.

❖ Margarine can be substituted for butter in all the recipes, but butter gives a fuller and richer flavour.

CAKES

SCRUMPTIOUS CHOCOLATE CAKE

As chocolate cakes go, this is the real thing, deliciously moist with a very rich chocolate flavour.

❖ Preheat the oven and line the bases of 2 x 20 cm (8") circular cake tins with greaseproof paper, brushing lightly with a little oil or melted butter to prevent sticking.

❖ Gently warm the butter until just melted, but not too hot. Place the caster sugar in the Kenwood Bowl, pour in the butter and use the K Beater at speed 3 to beat until light and fluffy.

❖ Crack the eggs into a pouring jug, beat with a fork and, while the K Beater is still turning, pour the eggs into the Bowl, a little at a time. The mixture should resemble a smooth batter.

❖ Incorporate the dissolved coffee, milk and almond essence into the batter. Add the ground almonds, then sieve the flour, baking powder and cocoa powder straight into the Bowl. Use the K Beater at minimum speed for as short a time as possible to combine these ingredients.

❖ Divide the cake mixture between the two tins (the Spatula does a good job of scraping the Bowl clean), smooth the tops and bake on the middle shelf for 30 minutes until springy to the touch. Cool on a wire rack. Fill and top the cake using the Chocolate Mousseline Filling .

225g (8oz, 1 cup) butter
250g (9oz, 1¼ cups) caster sugar
4 eggs
5ml (1 tsp) instant coffee, dissolved in 15ml (1 tbsp) hot water
30ml (2 tbsp) milk
5ml (1 tsp) almond essence
50g (2oz, ⅔ cup) ground almonds
100g (4oz, 1 cup) self raising flour
5ml (1 tsp) baking powder
50g (2oz, ½ cup) unsweetened cocoa powder

☐ *Oven Temperature 180°C (350°F, gas mark 4)*
◯ *Makes 1 x 20cm (8") cake for 8-10 servings*
✳ *Suitable for freezing, before icing*

CHOCOLATE MOUSSELINE FILLING

❖ Melt the chocolate pieces by placing in a bowl over a pan of barely simmering water.

❖ Using the Balloon Whisk beat the cream until soft peaks form when the Whisk is lifted away (see page 38 for hints and tips on whipping cream and egg whites).

❖ When the chocolate has melted remove the bowl from the heat and, using a large metal spoon, fold it into the cream. The filling is now ready for use.

275g (10oz) plain chocolate, broken into pieces
225ml (8fl oz, 1 cup) double cream

◯ *Makes enough to fill and top 1 x 20cm (8") circular cake*
✗ *Not suitable for freezing*

CELEBRATION FRUIT CAKE

A rich fruit cake which is suitable for any type of celebration, be it a wedding, christening, or birthday. Remember it needs to be started at least one day before it is required.

225g (8oz, 1½ cups) currants
225g (8oz, 1½ cups) raisins
225g (8oz, 1⅓ cups) dates, chopped
175g (6oz, 1 cup) sultanas
100g (4oz, ½ cup) glacé cherries, quartered
100g (4oz, ¾ cup) cut mixed peel
100g (4oz, ⅔ cup) whole blanched almonds, roughly chopped
175ml (6fl oz, ⅔ cup) brandy
250g (9oz, 1¼ cups) butter, at room temperature
100g (4oz, ⅔ cup) demerara sugar
150g (5oz, ⅔ cup) caster sugar
6 eggs, beaten
225g (8oz, 1¾ cups) plain flour
225g (8oz, 2⅔ cups) ground almonds
15ml (1 tbsp) cocoa powder
2.5ml (½ tsp) nutmeg, freshly grated
2.5ml (½ tsp) mixed spice
2.5ml (½ tsp) salt
zest of 1 orange and 1 lemon, grated
5ml (1 tsp) vanilla essence
greaseproof paper for lining the tin
brown paper for wrapping around the tin during cooking

☐ *Oven Temperature 150°C (300°F, gas mark 2)*
◯ *Makes 1 large 20cm (8") cake - enough for 30 people*
✗ *Not suitable for freezing*

❖ Put the currants, raisins, dates, sultanas, glacé cherries, mixed peel and chopped blanched almonds into a bowl. Pour in the brandy and give a quick stir to ensure it is all coated. Cover, then leave to soak in a cool place for 24 hours.

❖ Preheat the oven and line a 20cm (8") circular cake tin with a double layer of greaseproof paper, brushing first with a little oil.

❖ Place the butter and sugars in the Kenwood Bowl and mix with the K Beater at speed 2 until light and fluffy. This takes a good 5 minutes.

❖ Add the beaten eggs a little at a time, with the K Beater still turning, until they have all been mixed in and you are left with a smooth, thick batter.

❖ Stop mixing and add the remaining ingredients, including the soaked fruits. Mix again at speed 1 until well incorporated.

❖ Spoon the cake mixture into the prepared cake tin. Cover with a double layer of greaseproof paper in which you should first cut a hole 2cm (1") in diameter.

❖ Tie a band of brown paper around the outside of the tin (this prevents the outside of the cake from cooking too quickly) and bake on a low shelf for 3 hours.

❖ Test to see if the cake is cooked by inserting a skewer into the centre. If it is cooked, the skewer will come out clean, if not bake for a further 30 minutes and check again.

❖ Leave to cool in the tin, then when cold remove the cake, which should still be wrapped in the paper. Wrap in plastic film for up to 3 months, until required.

❖ The cake is now ready to be covered with Almond Paste and Snow Icing. It can however be eaten plain.

Almond Paste (Marzipan)

❖ Place all the ingredients in the Kenwood Bowl and mix with the K Beater at minimum speed until a dough-like consistency is achieved. Cover in plastic film until required for use.

❖ To cover the cake, roll out two thirds of the quantity of almond paste, using icing sugar to prevent sticking, to make a rectangle long enough and wide enough to coat the sides of the cake. Turn the cake upside down so that the top is nice and flat.

❖ Brush the cake top and sides with apricot jam which should first be warmed to make it easier to use, then stick the almond paste to the sides of the cake.

❖ Roll out the remaining almond paste to make a circle the size of the cake top. Lay it over the top and gently press down to ensure it is well adhered.

❖ The cake should now be left in an airy place for about 1 week to allow the almond paste to dry, before covering with a layer of Snow Icing.

450g (1lb, 5⅓ cups) ground almonds

175g (6oz, ¾ cup) caster sugar

225g (8oz, 1¼ cups) icing sugar, sifted

1 whole egg

2 egg yolks (reserve the whites for Snow Icing)

2.5ml (½ tsp) vanilla essence

2.5ml (½ tsp) almond essence

10ml (2 tsp) brandy

45ml (3 tbsp) apricot jam, for brushing the cake

○ *Makes enough to cover 1 x 20cm (8") fruit cake*

✗ *Not suitable for freezing*

Snow Icing

❖ Place the egg whites in the Kenwood Bowl and, with the K Beater running at minimum speed, add the icing sugar a spoon at a time.

❖ When all the icing sugar has been added, turn the speed up to 4 and beat the icing for 10 minutes to a smooth, thick consistency. Add the glycerine and mix thoroughly.

❖ Coat the cake with the icing mixture leaving the sides flat in case you wish to tie a ribbon around the outside. At this stage you can also create peaks by placing the flat side of the Spatula against the icing and pulling away swiftly.

❖ Let the icing dry for a day and then decorate for the appropriate celebration.

3 egg whites

450g (1lb, 3½ cups) icing sugar, sifted

5ml (1 tsp) glycerine

○ *Makes enough to cover 1 x 20cm (8") fruit cake*

✗ *Not suitable for freezing*

ELEVENSES CAKE

This is an almond-flavoured sponge with a hint of lemon, hiding a layer of not-too-sweet fruit preserve.
The whole cake is topped with crunchy demerara sugar and walnuts - just perfect for coffee time.

100g (4oz, ½ cup) butter
100g (4oz, ½ cup) sugar
2 eggs
5ml (1 tsp) almond essence
zest of 1 lemon, grated
15ml (1 tbsp) lemon juice
150g (5oz, ½ cup) plain yoghurt
225g (8oz, 1¼ cups) plain flour
2.5 ml (½ tsp) salt
10ml (2 tsp) baking powder
50g (2oz, ½ cup) walnut pieces
45ml (3 tbsp) redcurrant or cranberry jelly/preserve
15ml (1 tbsp) demerara sugar
75g (3oz, ¾ cup) walnut halves, for decoration

☐ *Oven Temperature 180°C (350°F, gas mark 4)*
○ *Makes 1 x 23cm (9") cake for 6-8 servings*
✳ *Suitable for freezing*

❖ Preheat the oven and line the base of a 23cm (9") circular cake tin with greaseproof paper, brushing it first with a little oil.

❖ Melt the butter gently and pour into the Kenwood Bowl with the sugar. Use the K Beater at speed 3 to beat the mixture until it is pale and fluffy.

❖ Beat the eggs in a jug and, while the Chef is still running, add the eggs a little at a time to the sugar and butter mixture until it resembles a smooth batter. Add the almond essence, lemon zest, lemon juice and yoghurt and mix at speed 1 until thoroughly combined.

❖ Switch off the Chef and add the flour, salt, baking powder, and walnut pieces. You can now use the K Beater as a gentle stirrer by switching to minimum speed and mixing thoroughly.

❖ Pour half the cake mixture into the prepared tin. Spoon over the redcurrant or cranberry jelly and smooth out with the Spatula.

❖ Pour the rest of the mixture over the top, sprinkle with the demerara sugar and decorate with the walnut halves.

❖ Bake in the oven for 30-40 minutes until an inserted skewer comes out clean. Leave in the tin for 5 minutes and then turn out and place on a wire rack to cool.

VANILLA CREAM CHEESECAKE

Cheesecake seems to be the popular food of New York, appearing at the tea table in many different guises. However one thing that all cheesecakes have in common is that they are rich, creamy and delicious. The fresh fruit topping offers the palate a complete contrast to the sweet, creamy centre and crunchy base.

❖ Preheat the oven and have ready a 23cm (9") circular cake tin which has a removable base, and has been lightly oiled.

❖ Crush the biscuits with the K Beater at speed 2 to form crumbs. This takes a couple of minutes.

❖ Meanwhile, melt the butter and pour onto the crushed biscuits while the K Beater is still turning. When all the butter has been evenly incorporated, tip the mixture into the cake tin and press down to form a flat surface.

❖ Clean the Bowl and put in the curd cheese, vanilla essence, eggs and sugar. Beat with the K Beater for 5 minutes.

❖ Add the double cream and mix until smooth. Pour onto the cooled biscuit mixture in the tin, then place in the oven and bake for 30 minutes.

❖ Switch off the oven and leave the cheesecake inside to cool very slowly. When cool, wrap in plastic film and refrigerate overnight. At this stage the cheesecake will last for up to 2 days.

❖ Just before serving, unwrap, place creamy side up on a plate and top with a mound of fresh fruits, arranged in a haphazard fashion.

225g (8oz, 2½ cups) digestive or sweetmeal biscuits

75g (3oz, ⅓ cup) butter

450g (1lb, 2 cups) curd cheese

5ml (1 tsp) vanilla essence

3 eggs

225g (8oz, 1 cup) caster sugar

225ml (8fl oz, 1 cup) double cream

450-900g (1-2lb) fresh soft fruits, such as strawberries, redcurrants, raspberries

☐ *Oven Temperature 180°C (350°F, gas mark 4)*

✪ *Serves 8-10*

✗ *Not suitable for freezing*

PASTRIES

PUFF PASTRY

Puff pastry, also known as 'Millefeuille' (a thousand leaves) is made from layers of pastry interlaced with butter. I have tried and tested many different recipes and this one is the result of combining the best from each.

225g (8oz, 1¾ cups) plain flour
225g (8oz, 1¾ cups) strong white flour
75g (3oz, ⅓ cup) butter, cubed
60ml (2fl oz, ¼ cup) vinegar
115ml (4fl oz, ½ cup) cold water
10ml (2 tsp) salt
2 egg yolks
400g (14oz, 1¾ cups) butter, chilled
50g (2oz, ½ cup) plain flour

○ *Makes 1.2kg (2lb 10oz) - equivalent to 5 standard quantities of 250g (9oz)*
❊ *Suitable for freezing*

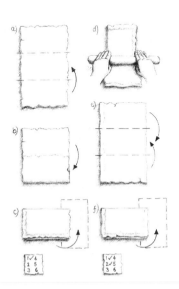

❖ Place the 225g (8oz, 1¾ cups) plain flour, the strong white flour and the 75g (3oz, ⅓ cups) cubed butter in the Kenwood Bowl. Use the K Beater at speed 1 to rub the butter and flour together.

❖ Mix together the vinegar, water, salt, and egg yolks in a jug. Using the Dough Hook at speed 1, add enough of this liquid until a soft, not sticky, dough has been formed. Leave to knead for 1 minute, then wrap in plastic film and set aside for 1 hour.

❖ Put the 400g (14oz, 1¾ cups) chilled butter into the Kenwood Bowl with the 50g (2oz, ½ cup) plain flour. Use the K Beater at minimum speed to work the flour into the butter. Pat the butter mixture into a flat block measuring roughly 18cm x 18cm (7" x 7") and leave to one side.

❖ Roll out the dough to a square measuring about 28cm x 28cm (11" x 11"). Place the butter pat in the centre and bring the sides of the pastry up and over to enclose the butter completely.

❖ Brush the edges with a little water to stick them down, then carefully roll out the dough to a rectangle roughly 50cm x 30cm (20" x 12"). Use flour on the underside to prevent sticking. Cover with a damp cloth and leave to rest for 1 hour.

❖ Brush the lower third with a little water and fold upwards. Brush the top third with a little water and fold this downwards, so that you have a neat parcel one third the size of the original rectangle. Give the dough a quarter turn to your left. To help you remember the number of folds, write the numbers 1 to 6 on a piece of paper, and tick off number 1.

❖ Roll out the dough again, not forgetting to sprinkle plenty of flour on the work surface to prevent sticking. Fold in the same way as before, giving the dough a quarter turn at the end. Tick off number 2.

❖ Leave the dough to rest for 30 minutes, covered with the damp cloth, before repeating this process twice more, and ticking off numbers 3 and 4.

- ❖ Cover with the cloth and let it rest for 1 hour. If at any stage butter is showing through the pastry, sprinkle a little flour over the spot and roll more gently!

- ❖ Repeat twice more, for stages 5 and 6. Your pastry is now ready for use. When cooking puff pastry the general rule is to chill it after it has been rolled, then sprinkle water on and around the pastry just before cooking in a very hot oven. The water turns to steam and helps the pastry rise even more.

- ❖ Puff Pastry can then be used for tart bases such as Tarte Tatin or made into individual pies or jam tarts decorated with a lattice topping.

TARTE TATIN

An apple tart which is baked upside-down, producing a delicious, caramel coating for the apples and a crisp layer of puff pastry.

- ❖ Preheat the oven. Roll out the puff pastry to a circle large enough to cover the surface of the frying pan.

- ❖ Peel the apples and slice them in half. Scoop out the core and coat the apple halves in the lemon juice. Spread the butter evenly over the bottom of the frying pan, then add the sugar, and shake around so that it too has an even coverage.

- ❖ Place the apples, flat side up, in the pan and lay the pastry over the top. Trim around the edges so that the pastry sits neatly just inside the frying pan.

- ❖ Now set the pan over a high heat and leave for about 10 minutes until a rich caramel colour is showing when you look under the pastry. Be careful, the steam is very hot.

- ❖ Put the whole pan into the oven and cook for a further 10-15 minutes, until the pastry is golden.

- ❖ Find a tray or plate which is at least 5cm (2") larger than the frying pan all the way round. Cover your arm with a teacloth, place the plate so that the top side faces down on top of the frying pan and quickly tip the tart on to the plate. Serve hot with double cream.

1 quantity of Puff Pastry, 250g (9oz)

6 dessert apples

juice of half a lemon

100g (4oz, ½ cup) butter

200g (7oz, 1 cup) sugar

heavy-based frying pan, 25cm (10") in diameter, which will also fit into the oven

- ☐ *Oven Temperature 190°C (375°F, gas mark 5)*
- ✿ *Serves 6*
- ✗ *Not suitable for freezing*

Rich Sweet Shortcrust Pastry

75g (3oz, ¾ cup) icing sugar
2 egg yolks
100g (4oz, ½ cup) butter, at room temperature, cut into pieces
250g (9oz, 2 cups) plain flour
pinch of salt
5ml (1 tsp) baking powder
30ml (2 tbsp) water

○ *Makes 1 quantity,*
2 x 23cm (9") tarts
✳ *Suitable for freezing*

❖ Put the icing sugar, egg yolks and butter into the Kenwood Bowl and using the K Beater, mix at speed 2 until they are creamed together. You may need to use the Spatula once or twice to scrape down any remaining butter from the top of the Bowl – always stop the Chef first when doing this.

❖ Sift together the flour, salt and baking powder and add to the Bowl.

❖ Mix to the consistency of breadcrumbs, then add the water and carry on mixing until the pastry is smooth.

❖ Wrap in plastic film and allow the pastry to rest in a cool place for at least 30 minutes before using.

Open Fruit Tart with Almond Cream Filling

½ quantity of Rich Sweet Shortcrust Pastry
50g (2oz, ½ cup) icing sugar
50g (2oz, ⅔ cup) ground almonds
1 egg
5ml (1 tsp) vanilla essence
30ml (2 tbsp) double cream
450g (1lb) soft fruits such as strawberries, kiwi fruit, seedless grapes
90ml (6 tbsp) apricot jam, sieved for glazing
30ml (2 tbsp) water

□ *Oven Temperature 180°C (350°F, gas mark 4)*
○ *Makes 1 x 23cm (9") tart*
✗ *Not suitable for freezing*

❖ Preheat the oven. Roll out the pastry to form a circle large enough to fit into a 23cm (9") tart tin. Use a little plain flour to prevent sticking.

❖ Line the tart tin with the pastry and chill well. Bake blind for 10-15 minutes until the pastry is barely coloured.

❖ To make the almond cream, combine the icing sugar, ground almonds, egg, vanilla essence and cream using the K Beater at minimum speed until the mixture becomes smooth.

❖ Pour into the pastry shell and bake for a further 10 minutes.

❖ Allow the tart to cool, unmould from the tin and place on a serving plate before decorating with the fruits.

❖ Heat the apricot jam with the water until it is just boiling. Allow to cool a little then brush the jam over the fruits to glaze them.

Oat & Wholemeal Shortcrust Pastry

❖ Put the flours, oatmeal, salt and butter into the Kenwood Bowl and, using the K Beater at speed 2, mix to the consistency of breadcrumbs.

❖ Sprinkle a little water, about 15ml (1 tbsp) at a time, into the Bowl, while the K Beater is still turning, until the pastry forms a dough.

❖ Wrap the pastry in plastic film and leave to rest in a cool place for about 30 minutes before using.

110g (4oz, 1 cup) wholemeal self raising flour

75g (3oz, ¼ cup) plain flour

25g (1oz, ¼ cup) medium oatmeal

pinch of salt

150g (5oz, ⅔ cup) butter, cut into pieces

water, for binding the pastry

○ *Makes 1 quantity, 1 large flan or 2 x 20cm (8") circular flans*

✳ *Suitable for freezing*

Cheese & Tomato Quiche

❖ Preheat the oven. Heat the butter over a medium heat and sauté the onion for about 10 minutes until soft but not coloured. Set aside until required.

❖ Meanwhile roll out the pastry into a circle large enough for lining a 24cm (9½") oiled flan tin. Use plenty of flour to prevent sticking.

❖ Line the tin with the pastry and bake the pastry blind for 15 minutes until crisp but not too coloured.

❖ While the pastry is cooking beat together the eggs, milk, mustard and seasoning.

❖ Take the pastry out of the oven and brush with a little of this egg mixture, then return to the oven for a further 5 minutes. This keeps the pastry crisp.

❖ Spread the sautéed onion over the base of the quiche, followed by the cheese and then pour over the egg mixture. Thinly slice the tomatoes and lay them on top to decorate.

❖ Bake for 25 minutes until the top is golden. Serve hot or cold with a large salad.

50g (1oz, ⅛ cup) butter or margarine

1 medium onion, peeled and finely sliced

1 quantity of Oat & Wholemeal Shortcrust Pastry

2 eggs

175ml (6fl oz, ⅔ cup) milk

5ml (1 tsp) mustard

salt and freshly milled black pepper

150g (5oz, 1⅓ cups) Cheddar or other similar cheese, grated

2 small tomatoes

☐ *Oven Temperature 180°C (350°F, gas mark 4)*

❂ *Serves 4-6*

✳ *Suitable for freezing*

ALMOND & ORANGE SWEET PASTRY

100g (4oz, 1 cup) plain flour

100g (4oz, 1⅓ cups) ground almonds

zest of 1 orange, grated

150g (5oz, ⅔ cup) butter, at room temperature, cut into pieces

25g (1oz, ⅛ cup) caster sugar

30ml (2 tbsp) orange juice

5ml (1 tsp) almond essence

○ *Makes 1 quantity, 18 individual pies or 1 large 24cm (9½") pie*

✳ *Suitable for freezing*

❖ Place the flour, almonds, orange zest and butter in the Kenwood Bowl.

❖ Use the K Beater at speed 1 to combine the ingredients until the mixture resembles breadcrumbs.

❖ Add the sugar, orange juice and almond essence and mix, adding a little cold water if necessary, until a smooth pastry has been formed.

❖ Wrap in plastic film and allow to rest in a cool place for 30 minutes before using.

LUXURY MINCE PIES

1 quantity of Almond & Orange Sweet Pastry

1 egg, beaten, for glazing

1 x 400g (14oz) jar mincemeat

☐ *Oven Temperature 190°C (375°F, gas mark 5)*

○ *Makes 18 mince pies*

✳ *Suitable for freezing*

❖ Preheat the oven. Roll out the pastry until it is about 2mm (⅒") in thickness. This pastry is quite fragile so be sure to use lots of flour when rolling out.

❖ Use an 8cm (3") circular cutter to press out the first 12 pastry bases.

❖ Put them in an oiled mince pie tray and brush the whole area of each with the beaten egg. This helps to keep the pastry crisp.

❖ Cut out 12 pastry lids using a 5cm (2") circular cutter.

❖ Put 5ml (1 tsp) mincemeat into each base and cover with a pastry lid. Press the lid around the outside to seal it well and brush with more egg to glaze. Repeat until all the pastry has been used, each time gathering up the scraps for re-rolling.

❖ Bake in the oven for 10-15 minutes until golden. Leave to cool in the tin for a couple of minutes before transferring to a wire rack.

❖ Store the mince pies in an airtight container.

... AND A WHOLE LOT MORE

BUTTERSCOTCH COOKIES

- ❖ Preheat the oven. Put the butter, sugar, salt, vanilla essence and egg into the Kenwood Bowl.
- ❖ Using the K Beater at speed 2, mix until the batter is smooth. This takes about 1 minute.
- ❖ Add the flour and chocolate chips and mix at minimum speed until all of the flour has been incorporated.
- ❖ Place small mounds of the mixture, approximately 15ml (1 tbsp) each, on an oiled baking sheet with about 5cm (2") between each mound.
- ❖ Bake for 6-8 minutes until just golden at the edges. Cool on the baking sheet for a few minutes before transferring to a wire rack.

225g (8oz, 1 cup) butter, at room temperature
100g (4oz, ⅔ cup) brown sugar
2.5ml (½ tsp) salt
2.5ml (½ tsp) vanilla essence
1 egg
175g (6oz, 1⅓ cups) plain flour
225g (8oz) dark chocolate, broken into small pieces

☐ *Oven Temperature 190°C (375°F, gas mark 5)*
◐ *Makes 16 cookies*
✗ *Not suitable for freezing*

SAVOURY SHORTBREAD

This shortbread has an excellent crunchy texture with a lovely tangy cheese flavour.
It is really good with hoummus (chickpea purée) and smoked mackerel pâté.

- ❖ Preheat the oven. Put the semolina, both flours, chilli powder, turmeric, mustard powder and butter into the Kenwood Bowl.
- ❖ Use the K Beater at speed 1 to work the mixture until it resembles breadcrumbs.
- ❖ Add the cheese, garlic and lemon juice and mix until all the ingredients are combined and a pastry is formed.
- ❖ Roll out on a lightly floured surface to a circle just larger than 23cm (9") in diameter. Use a tart tin to cut out a neat round.
- ❖ Place on an oiled baking sheet and bake for 20 minutes until just golden.
- ❖ Cool on the baking sheet, then cut into wedges and keep in an airtight container until required.

50g (2oz, ⅓ cup) semolina
50g (2oz, ½ cup) wholemeal flour
50g (2oz, ½ cup) plain white flour
2.5ml (½ tsp) chilli powder
2.5ml (½ tsp) turmeric
2.5ml (½ tsp) mustard powder
100g (4oz, ½ cup) butter, at room temperature
100g (4oz, 1⅓ cups) cheese, such as Cheddar, grated
1 clove garlic, crushed
juice of 1 lemon

☐ *Oven Temperature 180°C (350°F, gas mark 4)*
◐ *Makes 6-8 wedges*
✗ *Not suitable for freezing*

MINI BRIE BRIOCHES

It is rumoured that the word 'brioche' originates from the famous cheese making region of France, known as Brie, where the local bread was first made using Brie cheese. I'm not sure whether this recipe tastes anything like its ancestor but these little brioches are extremely good. Traditionally this dough kneading would have been done with a spoon - they must have had such strong arms!

225g (8oz, 1¼ cups) strong white flour

5ml (1 tsp) easy-blend yeast (see p.30 for yeast conversion)

15ml (1 tbsp) sugar

5ml (1 tsp) salt

2 eggs

60ml (2fl oz, ¼ cup) milk, warmed

100g (4oz) Brie cheese, cut into small pieces

175g (6oz, ¾ cup) butter, at room temperature

☐ *Oven Temperature 200°C (400°F, gas mark 6)*
○ *Makes 12 brioches*
✗ *Not suitable for freezing*

❖ Put the flour, yeast, sugar, salt, eggs and milk into the Kenwood Bowl and, using the K Beater, beat at a low speed for 5 minutes. The mixture will be of a sticky consistency.

❖ Add the Brie cheese and butter and carry on mixing, with the K Beater at a low speed, for a further 5 minutes.

❖ Remove the Bowl with the dough inside and cover with some oiled plastic film, then leave in a warm place to rise. The high fat content and relatively low yeast content means quite a slow rising. It will take at least 2 hours to double its size.

❖ When the dough is nicely risen, push it down again using the plastic film so that your fingers don't get stuck to the dough.

❖ Put the dough into a small bowl and place in the refrigerator. Leave for at least 6 hours or overnight, but no longer than 24 hours.

❖ Remove the dough from the bowl (by now it will have lost its stickiness) and split into 12 pieces, then form into 12 balls. Put each one into a mini brioche tin and leave to rise again in a warm place. This will take 1½ hours.

❖ Bake in a preheated oven for 15 minutes until golden. Serve warm with ham, cheese or soup.

POTATO FOCACCIA BREAD

The K Beater makes perfectly smooth mashed potato in seconds. This recipe is quick to make and excellent for lunch. Try it with a topping of cherry tomatoes, anchovies, capers or one of your own favourites.

❖ Peel the potatoes and dice into 4cm (1½") cubes. Put them in a pan with the salt and pour in boiling water to cover. Simmer for 10 minutes until tender.

❖ Drain the potatoes, allow to cool for 10 minutes, then place in the Kenwood Bowl. Use the K Beater at speed 2 to mash until the potato is smooth.

❖ Add the flour, yeast, salt, and olive oil then mix at speed 1, adding enough water to form a dough.

❖ Replace the K Beater with the Dough Hook and knead at speed 1 for 5 minutes until smooth and elastic.

❖ Remove the Bowl with the dough inside, cover loosely with plastic film and leave to rise. This takes less than an hour because of the warmth from the mashed potatoes.

❖ Preheat the oven and oil a 23cm (9") pie tin. When the dough has doubled its size transfer it to the prepared tin where it will lose some of its puffiness.

❖ Use a finger to make 8 deep impressions in the dough and put either a small amount, 5ml (1 tsp) of Neapolitan-style sauce or half a cherry tomato in each.

❖ Sprinkle the top with dried basil and salt, and bake in the oven for 50 minutes until golden brown.

❖ Leave to cool for a few minutes, then turn out of the tin and serve hot with a large salad.

325g (12oz) potatoes
10ml (2 tsp) salt
boiling water, for cooking
450g (1lb, 3½ cups) strong white bread flour
10ml (2 tsp) easy-blend yeast, (see p.30 for yeast conversion)
10ml (2 tsp) salt
30ml (2 tbsp) olive oil
175ml (6fl oz, ⅔ cup) water
olive oil, for oiling the pie tin
40ml (8 tsp) ready-made Neapolitan-style sauce, or cherry tomatoes, halved
5ml (1 tsp) dried basil
1.25ml (¼ tsp) salt, for sprinkling over the top

☐ *Oven Temperature 200°C (400°F, gas mark 6)*
✪ *Serves 4-6*
✳ *Suitable for freezing*

IRISH SODA BREAD

Apart from being superb bread for a yeast-free diet this is a particularly good recipe if you have no time to wait for yeast bread to rise. It is simple and delicious and when cooked resembles an over-sized scone.

45ml (3 tbsp, ¼ cup) oats
325g (12oz, 2¾ cups) 100% wholemeal bread flour
100g (4oz, 1 cup) plain flour
2.5ml (½ tsp) baking powder
2.5ml (½ tsp) bicarbonate of soda
2.5ml (½ tsp) salt
1 egg
75g (3oz, ⅓ cup) natural yoghurt
30ml (2 tbsp) vegetable oil
300ml (½ pint, 1¼ cups) fresh milk

☐ *Oven Temperature 180°C (350°F, gas mark 4)*
○ *Makes 1 medium-sized loaf*
✳ *Suitable for freezing*

❖ Preheat the oven. Oil a bread tin with base measurements 19cm x 9cm (7½" x 3½"), shaking 30ml (2 tbsp) of the oats around the base and sides so that they are evenly coated. This prevents the bread sticking and gives it a really oaty flavour.

❖ Place all the dry ingredients in the Kenwood Bowl.

❖ Mix the egg, yoghurt, oil and milk together in a jug.

❖ Using the K Beater at speed 2 combine all the dry ingredients and then add the yoghurt mixture. Carry on mixing until well combined.

❖ Press into the prepared tin, sprinkle the top with the remaining oats and bake on the middle shelf of an oven for about 50-60 minutes, until an inserted skewer comes out clean.

❖ Turn out of the tin and place on a wire rack to cool.

SWEET IRISH SODA BREAD

100g (4oz, 1 cup) raisins
150ml (¼ pint, ½ cup) hot water, not boiling
450g (1lb, 3½ cups) white bread flour
5ml (1 tsp) salt
5ml (1 tsp) baking powder
25g (1oz, ⅛ cup) sugar
15ml (1 tbsp) caraway seeds
1 egg
150ml (¼ pint, ½ cup) yoghurt
150ml (¼ pint, ½ cup) milk

☐ *Oven Temperature 180°C (350°F, gas mark 4)*
○ *Makes 1 medium-sized loaf*
✳ *Suitable for freezing*

❖ Soak the raisins in the water for 10 minutes to soften them.

❖ Preheat the oven. Oil a bread tin with base measurements 19cm x 9cm (7½" x 3½"), shaking a little flour around the base and sides to prevent sticking.

❖ Drain the raisins and discard the water. Place all the ingredients in the Kenwood Bowl and, using the K Beater, mix on speed 2 for 1 minute until well combined.

❖ Press into the bread tin and bake for 1 hour or until an inserted skewer comes out clean.

❖ Turn out of the tin and place on a wire rack to cool.

Clockwise, from top left:

Celebration Fruit Cake

Vanilla Cream Cheesecake

Irish Soda Bread

Puff Pastry Lattice Jam Tarts

Tarte Tatin

Scrumptious Chocolate Cake

HOME-BAKED BREAD - THE SIMPLE WAY

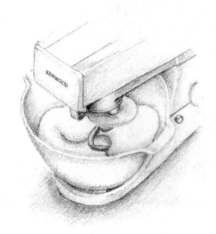

How truly comforting are the smells of new bread, so rich, warm and yeasty. The wonderful texture of silky dough, puffing up in the warmth. Then that crowning moment when the loaves are removed from the oven - rounded, golden and perfectly textured. Oh! How a simple thing can make a home such a happy place.

Making bread is still one of the most popular uses for the Kenwood Chef with many households, especially in Scandinavia using the Chef mostly for that purpose. The reason is obvious - the Dough Hook's capability in handling the ingredients, combining them with an even distribution then kneading them into the most perfectly smooth and springy dough with almost no effort from yourself is, without doubt, a real asset to the kitchen.

The results are always excellent. This, so I am told, is to do with the unique planetary action which enables the Dough Hook to be gentle yet firm with the dough, rather like the traditional 'kneading by hand' method. The Chef will happily make small or very large batches of bread, your hands not having to touch the dough until it is time to put it in the baking tin. As well as excellent breads the Dough Hook will also make dough for rolls, buns, pizzas and pasta for pasta rollers.

Bread freezes beautifully. As soon as it is cooled, wrap it in plastic film and place it in the freezer. Before required, unwrap and leave for a couple of hours for the bread to defrost.

All the recipes in the following pages include the use of easy-blend yeast. Below is a table showing the different quantities for easy-blend, active dried and fresh yeast as well as the methods for their use.

yeast type	easy-blend yeast	active dried yeast	fresh yeast
Comparable quantities of yeast	1 Sachet 12.5ml (2½ tsp)	7g (¼ oz)	14g (½ oz)
Method	Mix into dry flour and proceed with recipe	Follow instructions on packet and add to dry ingredients with the liquid	Stir correct amount into the warm liquid and use straight away

N.B. To achieve best results, all recipes in this section should be used only with the quantities stated. For recipes using larger quantities of ingredients, it is advisable to consult the instruction leaflet included in your Kitchen Machine.

MIXED WHOLEGRAIN LOAF

❖ Put all the ingredients in the Kenwood Bowl except the water. Using the Dough Hook at minimum speed gradually add the water to the flour until a soft dough has been formed. Not all the water may be required.

❖ Allow to knead for 10 minutes, still at minimum speed. Remove the Bowl with the dough inside and cover it loosely with plastic film, then leave to rise in a warm place until doubled in size (about 1-2 hours).

❖ Preheat the oven. Re-knead the dough, using the Dough Hook, for 1 minute at minimum speed, and place in an oiled bread tin.

❖ Allow to puff up for a further 30 minutes, then bake for 30 minutes until the bread sounds hollow when tapped on its base. Leave to cool on a wire rack .

75g (3oz, ¼ cup) stoneground wholemeal bread flour
175g (6oz, 1⅓ cups) plain flour
75g (3oz, ⅔ cup) rye flour
50g (2oz, ⅓ cup) medium oatmeal
50g (2oz, ½ cup) sesame seeds
50g (2oz, ⅓ cup) sunflower seeds
10ml (2 tsp) salt
1 sachet easy-blend yeast, (see p.30 for yeast conversion)
10ml (2 tsp) brown sugar
15ml (1 tbsp) salad oil
300ml (½ pint, 1¼ cups) warm water

☐ *Oven Temperature 190°C (375°F, gas mark 5)*
◯ *Makes 1 medium-sized loaf*
✳ *Suitable for freezing*

RYE BREAD

This is a small close-textured loaf which is excellent for cheese and soups. I love it toasted with honey.

❖ Simply put all the ingredients into the Kenwood Bowl except the water. Use the Dough Hook at minimum speed, adding enough water to make a soft dough.

❖ Knead, still at minimum speed, for 10 minutes. Remove the Bowl with the dough inside and cover it loosely with plastic film. Leave to rise in a warm place until doubled in size (about 1-2 hours).

❖ Preheat the oven. Mould the dough into a loaf shape and place on a baking sheet. Cover again and leave to rise a second time for about 30-60 minutes.

❖ Bake for 20 minutes until the bread sounds hollow when tapped on its base. Leave to cool on a wire rack.

100g (4oz, ¼ cup) rye flour
50g (2oz, ½ cup) wholemeal bread flour
50g (2oz, ½ cup) white bread flour
50g (2oz, ⅓ cup) coarse cornmeal
5ml (1 tsp) caraway seeds
7.5ml (1½ tsp) salt
15ml (1 tbsp) vegetable oil
5ml (1 tsp) easy-blend yeast, (see p.30 for yeast conversion)
7.5ml (1½ tsp) sugar
175ml (6fl oz, ⅔ cup) warm water

☐ *Oven Temperature 190°C (375°F, gas mark 5)*
◯ *Makes 1 small loaf*
✳ *Suitable for freezing*

ZOPF (SWISS SUNDAY BREAD)

150ml (¼ pint, ½ cup) milk

75g (3oz, ⅓ cup) butter

450g (1lb, 3½ cups) white bread flour

1 sachet easy-blend yeast, (see p.30 for yeast conversion)

25g (1oz, ⅛ cup) sugar

10ml (2 tsp) salt

1 egg

1 egg yolk, for glazing

□ Oven Temperature 180°C (350°F, gas mark 4)

○ Makes 1 large loaf

✳ Suitable for freezing

❖ Heat the milk and butter together until the butter is melted and the milk is just warm.

❖ Place the remaining ingredients, except the egg yolk, in the Kenwood Bowl and use the Dough Hook at minimum speed to form a dough while pouring the milk mixture over the dry ingredients. You may need a drop more milk if the dough is too dry.

❖ Knead for 10 minutes, still at minimum speed.

❖ Remove the Bowl with the dough inside and cover it loosely with plastic film, then leave to rise in a warm place until doubled in size, (about 1 -2 hours).

❖ Preheat the oven. Use the Dough Hook a second time for 1 minute to re-knead the dough.

❖ Split the dough into three equal pieces, rolling each into a long sausage shape, and lay them side by side.

❖ Starting at one end, plait by folding the outside sausage over the middle one, alternating sides as you go.

❖ Lay the bread on a lightly oiled baking sheet, cover again with the plastic film and leave for about 30 minutes to puff up. Just before baking, brush with the egg yolk.

❖ Bake in the oven for about 30 minutes until the bread sounds hollow when tapped on its base and the top has turned golden brown.

PROSCIUTTO & PARMESAN BREAD

This bread is so utterly delicious - all it needs is a thin scraping of butter and, when served with a large salad, is perfect for lunch.

❖ Put all the dry ingredients in the Kenwood Bowl. Mix the eggs, olive oil and water together and, while the Dough Hook is turning at minimum speed, pour the liquid into the Bowl.

❖ Knead for 5 minutes, until smooth and elastic, adding a little more flour or water if necessary to make a soft dough.

❖ Remove the Bowl with the dough inside and cover it loosely with plastic film to allow enough room for expansion, then leave to rise in a warm place until doubled in size (usually about 1 hour).

❖ Use the Dough Hook to re-knead the dough for 1 minute and then shape it into two oblong loaves, rather like baguettes.

❖ Preheat the oven. Sprinkle a baking sheet with some of the cornmeal, lay the loaves not too close together and then sprinkle the tops with more cornmeal.

❖ Leave to rise for a further 30 minutes or until well risen, but not quite doubled in size. Use a very sharp knife to make six slashes diagonally across the top of each loaf.

❖ Bake for 25 minutes until the bread sounds hollow when tapped on its base and the surface is golden. Leave to cool on a wire rack.

450g (1lb, 3½ cups) strong white bread flour

1 sachet easy-blend yeast, (see p.30 for yeast conversion)

7.5ml (1½ tsp) salt

2.5ml (½ tsp) black pepper, freshly milled

50g (2oz, ½ cup) Parmesan cheese, freshly grated

50g (2oz, ½ cup) prosciutto ham, finely chopped, or sun-dried tomatoes, finely chopped

2 eggs

30ml (2 tsp) olive oil

150ml (¼ pint, ½ cup) water, hand hot

cornmeal for dusting

☐ *Oven Temperature 200°C (400°F, gas mark 6)*

◯ *Makes 2 small baguettes*

✳ *Suitable for freezing*

FRYING PAN NAAN BREAD

It took several attempts and a trip to an Indian Restaurant in London before I realised that the Tandoor oven could never be recreated at home - no matter how hot the oven gets. So I developed this alternative method, using a frying pan instead. I think these are so delicious that I prefer them to the traditional naan bread.

25g (1oz, ⅛ cup) butter
150ml (¼ pint, ½ cup) milk
400g (14oz, 3¼ cups) strong white bread flour
15ml (1 tbsp) cumin seeds
5ml (1 tsp) baking powder
7.5ml (1½ tsp) easy-blend yeast, (see p.30 for yeast conversion)
20ml (4 tsp) sugar
1 egg
15ml (1 tbsp) salad oil
10ml (2 tsp) salt
50g (2oz, ⅓ cup) butter, for brushing

○ *Makes 8 naan bread*
✳ *Suitable for freezing*

❖ Heat together the butter and milk until the butter has melted and the milk is no more than hand-hot.

❖ Put all the other ingredients in the Kenwood Bowl and, using the Dough Hook at minimum speed, make into a soft dough, pouring in the milk mixture as the Chef is running. If the dough is too dry add a little more milk. Knead for 10 minutes.

❖ Remove the Bowl with the dough inside and cover it loosely with plastic film. Leave to rise in a warm place until doubled in size.

❖ Split the dough into 8 pieces and place on a floured tray near the cooker. Melt the butter and keep nearby with a pastry brush, ready to use. Heat a heavy-based frying pan over a moderately high heat.

❖ Take one piece of the dough and pull it out into a rough circle just larger than the size of your hand. Now hold it in one hand while you brush the pan with a little melted butter.

❖ Toss the naan into the pan and let it fry on this side for 2 minutes. Meanwhile brush the top with some more melted butter.

❖ Turn the naan bread over and cook for a further 1½ minutes. Brush the cooked side with more butter, then proceed with the remaining dough balls.

❖ Serve hot or as soon as they are cool, wrap well in plastic film and freeze. Before serving, unwrap and heat through.

BAGELS

Bagels are traditionally filled with smoked salmon, cream cheese, a squeeze of lemon juice and a grind of black pepper. They cost surprisingly little - one bagel on its own is pretty filling, and you can be sparing on the smoked salmon. I went to a traditional bread shop in Brick Lane, London to find out the secret of making a great bagel.

❖ In the Kenwood Bowl, and with the Dough Hook fitted, mix together the flour, malt extract (or sugar), salt and yeast. While the Dough Hook is still turning at minimum speed, pour in enough warm water to form a dough. You may not need the whole quantity.

❖ Carry on kneading at minimum speed for 7 minutes until the dough is smooth and elastic.

❖ Remove the Bowl with the dough inside and cover it loosely with plastic film so that there is room for expansion. Leave to rise in a warm place for 1 hour or until it has doubled in size.

❖ Using the Dough Hook knead the dough again for 2 minutes and then split into 12 equal pieces.

❖ Make each piece into a ball, using extra flour if sticky, and make a hole in the middle so that each one looks like a ring doughnut.

❖ Place each bagel on a floured baking sheet and leave to one side for 30 minutes. Meanwhile bring to the boil a large pan of water and preheat the oven.

❖ Drop batches of the bagels (2 or 3 at a time) into the boiling water and simmer for 2 minutes. Then turn them over and simmer for a further 1½ minutes. Remove with a slotted spoon and drain on a wire rack.

❖ When all the bagels have had a 'hot bath' put them on oiled baking sheets, brush with the beaten egg and bake in the oven for 12 minutes.

❖ Turn the bagels over and bake for a further 5 minutes until golden brown.

❖ Serve when still warm with cream cheese, smoked salmon, a squeeze of lemon juice and a grind of black pepper.

❖ Other fillings could be used such as tuna, grated cheese or whatever you like!

450g (1lb, 3½ cups) strong white bread flour

15ml (1 tbsp) malt extract or brown sugar

15ml (1 tbsp) salt

1 sachet easy-blend yeast, (see p.30 for yeast conversion)

300ml (½ pint, 1¼ cups) warm water

1 egg, beaten, for glazing

☐ *Oven Temperature 200°C (400°F, gas mark 6)*
○ *Makes 12 bagels*
✳ *Suitable for freezing*

Mediterranean Fruit Bread

This recipe originates from the traditional bread baked for the Greek Easter. It would be decorated with brightly-coloured hard-boiled eggs which had been nestled in the dough just before baking, and sometimes a few coins would be hidden inside the dough for a surprise.

450g (1lb, 3½ cups) strong white bread flour

5ml (1 tsp) ground cinnamon

2.5ml (½ tsp) ground ginger

60ml (4 tbsp) olive oil

50g (2oz, ½ cup) mixed nuts, chopped

50g (2oz, ¼ cup) caster sugar

75g (3oz, ½ cup) sultanas,

zest of half a lemon, finely grated

2.5ml (½ tsp) salt

2 sachets easy-blend yeast, (see p.30 for yeast conversion)

300ml (½ pint, 1¼ cups) milk, hand hot

1 egg, beaten, for glazing

☐ *Oven Temperature 200°C (400°F, gas mark 6)*

◯ *Makes 1 large ring or 12 buns*

✳ *Suitable for freezing*

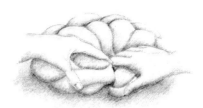

❖ Sift the flour and spices into the Kenwood Bowl, then add the olive oil, chopped mixed nuts, caster sugar, sultanas, lemon zest, salt and easy-blend yeast.

❖ Use the K Beater to combine all the ingredients. Now replace the K Beater with the Dough Hook and set to minimum speed.

❖ Pour in the milk until a soft dough is formed. Different flours need varying quantities of liquid to achieve the same results, so you may not need all of the milk. Allow the Dough Hook to knead the dough at minimum speed for 7 minutes until it is smooth and elastic.

❖ Remove the Bowl with the dough inside and cover it loosely with a generous amount of plastic film, so that there is enough room for the dough to rise, then leave it in a warm place until doubled in size. It takes about 1-1½ hours, unless your home is cold, in which case it can take longer.

❖ Preheat the oven. Remove the plastic film and, using the Dough Hook once again, knead the dough at speed 1 for another 60 seconds.

❖ If you are making a loaf, split the dough into 3 equal pieces, rolling each into a long sausage shape, then lay them side by side. Starting at one end, plait by folding the outside sausage over the middle one, alternating sides as you go. Lay the plait on a baking sheet, joining the ends together so that it forms a circle.

❖ If you are making buns, simply divide into 12 and mould into rounds.

❖ Brush the surface of the dough with a little beaten egg to glaze, cover it loosely with the plastic film and allow to rise for about 30 minutes in a warm place, or about 1 hour at room temperature.

❖ The dough is then ready to bake. Baking times are: 30 minutes for a plaited loaf and 12 minutes for buns. To test the bread simply tap on the underside. When it is cooked it will sound hollow. Cool on a wire rack, then serve sliced and buttered.

Basket:

*Mediterranean Fruit
Buns*

———

*Prosciutto & Parmesan
Bread*

———

*Zopf
(Swiss Sunday Bread)*

———

Mini Brie Brioches

Tray:

*Mediterranean Fruit
Bread*

———

Rye Bread

———

Frying Pan Naan Bread

Board:

Bagels

———

Mixed Wholegrain Loaf

WHISKING, WHIPPING & FOAMING

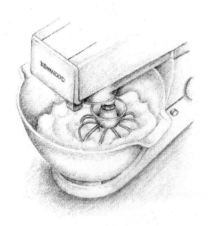

A great chef will always carefully consider the balance of a menu, being aware not only of combining flavours, but also colour and texture - it's important to keep a gastronome's interest throughout the whole meal. Something soft and foaming, such as soufflé or sabyon, creates a great contrast to something crisp and crunchy. The Balloon Whisk is brilliant for creating foamy mixtures and has a wonderful shape which is so conducive to creating maximum volume.

Even one single egg white can be used to create great volume, which is why so many professionals around the world use the Chef for the task of whipping small amounts of fresh cream.

When you begin whisking an egg white, you firstly get a light runny foam. The foam gradually becomes stiffer and the volume increases, yet it still has a wet appearance. This is called the soft peak stage and is the stage usually called for in recipes. To check, lift the Whisk from the foam so that a little remains on the Whisk, and then tip it up. The foam should maintain its shape, but the peak should flop.

If you carry on whisking, the foam will become even stiffer and will take on a dry appearance. You will then be able to tip the bowl upside-down without anything falling out! At this stage you have whisked the egg white to its fullest capacity, and if you whisk any more it will deflate.

Cream whisks in very much the same way as egg whites. Overwhisk it by a few seconds and you'll be on your way to making butter. As well as cream and egg white, there are a whole host of recipes that you can make with the Balloon Whisk, from mayonnaise and meringue to mousse and passion cake, as you'll see on the forthcoming pages.

HINTS & TIPS

❖ When whisking egg whites make sure your bowl is scrupulously clean - wipe it with half a lemon to make sure.

❖ When you are folding ingredients into the whipped cream or egg whites use either a large metal spoon or the Spatula and be very gentle so as not to deflate the bubbles.

❖ The Stainless Steel Bowl encourages egg whites to whisk faster and helps keep your ingredients cool.

❖ If you have a Splashguard remove it for whisking so as not to prevent the air from circulating.

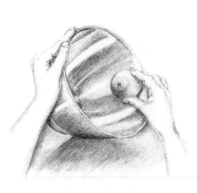

Cajun Style Hot Crab Soufflé

This is a twice-baked soufflé which means you can bake it in advance and then cook it a second time when you want to use it. Served on a bed of salad and topped with Greek-style yoghurt, it makes a simply stunning first course.

❖ Preheat the oven. Separate the eggs, placing the whites straight in the Kenwood Bowl and setting aside the yolks. Melt the butter over a fairly low heat and, when it is just bubbling, add the flour. Stir constantly until you have a smooth paste.

❖ Remove the pan from the heat and let it cool a little before you add the milk, stirring quickly to produce a smooth sauce. Return the pan to the heat and bring to simmering point, stirring constantly, so that the sauce thickens.

❖ Remove from the heat once more and stir in the crab, Cheddar cheese, anchovy essence, Cajun spices, egg yolks and lime juice.

❖ Oil 6 ramekins and place them in a roasting pan.

❖ Using the Whisk at maximum speed, whisk the egg whites until they form soft peaks. Now very gently fold the egg whites into the crab mixture taking care not to beat. You are trying to leave as much air as possible inside.

❖ When the mixture is ready, pour it into the ramekins. Pour boiling water into the roasting tray, around the ramekins, to a depth of about 2.5cm (1").

❖ Bake for 25 minutes until the soufflés are risen with a springy consistency. It is important not to undercook the soufflés.

❖ Leave the soufflés in the ramekins and place on a wire rack to cool. They will subside at this stage. The soufflés can now be refrigerated and covered in plastic film, for up to 2 days, or frozen.

❖ When you are ready to serve, preheat the oven to the same temperature as before. Remove the soufflés from the ramekins and place on a buttered baking sheet.

❖ Sprinkle the Parmesan cheese over the top and bake for 10 minutes. Serve with 5ml (1 tsp) Greek-style yoghurt spooned over each, and a small salad.

2 eggs

25g (1oz, ⅛ cup) butter

25g (1oz, ¼ cup) self raising flour

225ml (8fl oz, 1 cup) milk

70g (2½ oz) dressed crab, canned or fresh

50g (2oz, ⅔ cup) Cheddar cheese, grated

10ml (2 tsp) anchovy essence

10ml (2 tsp) Cajun spices, the ready-mixed type

10ml (2 tsp) lime juice

30ml (2 tbsp) Parmesan cheese, freshly grated

30ml (6 tsp) Greek-style natural yoghurt, for serving

☐ *Oven Temperature 190°C (375°F, gas mark 5)*

○ *Makes 6 small soufflés*

✳ *Freezes well before the last baking - but do make sure it is thoroughly defrosted before commencing with the rest of the recipe*

OLIVE OIL MAYONNAISE

Mayonnaise is an exceptional accompaniment to hard-boiled eggs, fish and cold meats as well as being the foundation to other classic sauces. However, there always seems to be a real fuss made over the preparation of real mayonnaise- probably because if you don't possess an electric whisk you need an arm made of steel to emulsify it. This recipe is a foolproof one - try it for yourself and discover the benefits of mayonnaise made the Kenwood way!

2 egg yolks
5ml (1 tsp) pale mustard
150ml (¼ pint, ½ cup) olive oil
150ml (¼ pint, ½ cup) vegetable oil
squeeze of lemon juice
salt and freshly milled white pepper
15ml (1 tbsp) white wine vinegar

○ *Makes 300 ml (½ pint, 1¼ cups)*
✗ *Not suitable for freezing*

❖ Place the egg yolks and mustard in the Kenwood Bowl. Then, before you begin whisking, mix the oils together. It is a good idea to use a jug which pours easily or alternatively you can use a spoon for adding the oil.

❖ Start whisking at maximum speed and when the egg has combined with the mustard, pour or spoon in the oil a few drops at a time.

❖ When you have poured in half the quantity of oil, switch off the Chef and add the lemon juice and some seasoning.

❖ The mayonnaise should now be thick and quite smooth. Resume the Whisk to maximum speed and slowly trickle in the oil.

❖ Add the vinegar and taste for seasoning. Spoon the mayonnaise into a clean jar, ready to use.

CURRIED MAYONNAISE

❖ Add 10ml (2 tsp) curry powder and 10ml (2 tsp) honey to half the quantity of the Olive Oil Mayonnaise recipe.

CORIANDER & LIME MAYONNAISE

❖ Substitute lime juice for the white wine vinegar, use all vegetable oil, 300ml (½ pint 1¼ cups) instead of olive oil and stir in 30ml (2 tbsp) chopped fresh coriander at the end.

TARRAGON & PINE NUT MAYONNAISE

❖ To a quarter of the quantity of the Olive Oil Mayonnaise Recipe, add 15ml (1 tbsp) chopped, fresh tarragon leaves and 30ml (2 tbsp) chopped pine nuts, which have been lightly toasted under the grill.

HOME-MADE BUTTER

During the making of butter, the cream splits into butter solids and buttermilk - the latter is often used in beauty treatments.

❖ Place the double cream in the Kenwood Bowl and use the Whisk at speed 3 until the cream is whipped beyond being thick, and starts to separate.

❖ Keep whisking until the butter solids separate completely from the liquid. Scoop the solids into a sieve to drain or else place in a muslin cloth, then squeeze the excess liquid with your hands.

❖ Pat the butter into a rectangle, or mould into balls. If flavouring, add ingredients before shaping it. Wrap the butter in foil or plastic film and chill until required.

SALTED BUTTER

❖ Use the K Beater to beat in 2.5ml (½ tsp) salt to the above quantity of Home-made Butter.

HERB BUTTER

❖ Use the K Beater to beat in 10ml (2 tsp) finely chopped, fresh herbs to the above quantity of fresh Home-made Salted Butter. The herbs could be a mixture of parsley, basil, or chives.

575ml (1 pint, 2¼ cups) double cream

fine mesh sieve or a square of muslin cloth

○ *Makes 1 pat of butter weighing approximately 225g (8oz)*

✳ *Suitable for freezing*

CHICKEN & LEEK STUFFED PANCAKES

PANCAKE BATTER:

50g (2oz, ½ cup) plain flour
pinch of salt
15ml (1 tbsp) butter, melted
1 egg
175ml (6fl oz, ⅔ cup) milk
butter or oil, for frying

FILLING:

15ml (1 tbsp) butter, for frying
325g (12oz) chicken, skin and bones removed, cut into small pieces
225g (8oz) mushrooms, thinly sliced
1 large leek, thinly sliced
nutmeg, salt and freshly milled pepper, for seasoning
25g (1oz, ⅛ cup) butter
25g (1oz, ¼ cup) plain flour
175ml (6fl oz, ⅔ cup) milk
100g (4oz, 1⅓ cups) Gruyère cheese, grated
150ml (¼ pint, ½ cup) double cream

□ *Oven Temperature 220°C (425°F, gas mark 7)*
○ *Makes 4 large pancakes for a main course or 8 small pancakes for a first course*
❊ *Suitable for freezing*

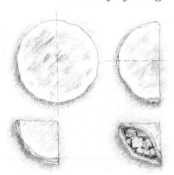

❖ To make the pancakes, put the flour, salt, melted butter and egg in the Kenwood Bowl and, using the Whisk at speed 1, mix until smooth.

❖ Add the milk, a little at a time, while the Whisk is still turning, to make a smooth batter. Pour into a jug ready for use and allow to rest for 30 minutes.

❖ Heat a pancake pan or frying pan over a fairly high heat and brush with a little melted butter or oil. Pour in some of the batter, swirling it around the pan to make a very thin, even coating. Cook for a couple of minutes until the edges are golden.

❖ Use a fish slice to turn the pancake, or toss if you feel daring! Return to the heat for 30 seconds so that the underside becomes golden, then slide onto a plate. Repeat to make 4 large or 8 small pancakes (depending on whether you are serving them as a first or main course), stacking them on top of each other.

❖ To make the filling, heat the butter in a heavy frying pan until very hot. Add the chicken pieces and stir-fry for 1 minute.

❖ Add the mushrooms and sliced leek and season well with nutmeg, salt and black pepper. Stir-fry for a further 5 minutes until the sliced leek is tender and the liquid has evaporated. Remove from the heat and allow to cool while you make the sauce.

❖ Heat the butter in a small pan and when it starts to foam, add the flour. Fry for 1 minute and remove from the heat. When it has cooled a little, add the milk and stir until smooth. Return to the heat and stir until the sauce thickens and simmers. Add to the chicken mixture and season again with the nutmeg, salt and pepper. Allow to cool before filling the pancakes.

❖ Preheat the oven. Divide the mixture evenly between the pancakes. You can either spoon it onto the flat pancake and tightly roll it up around the mixture, or firstly fold the pancake into quarters and stuff the mixture into one of the pockets. You can now freeze these pancakes, but defrost them well before baking.

❖ When required, place in a well-buttered ovenproof dish and sprinkle with the Gruyère cheese and cream. Bake for 25 minutes until it is piping hot and the cheese has turned a golden colour. Serve with a large green salad.

ALMOND PAVLOVA WITH SUMMER FRUITS

❖ Preheat the oven. Make sure the Kenwood Bowl is very clean - any traces of grease will prevent the egg whites from foaming fully. Place the baking parchment on a baking sheet.

❖ Place the egg whites in the Kenwood Bowl with the salt and lemon juice. Use the Whisk at speed 5 until the egg whites start to form soft peaks and they still have a wet appearance.

❖ While the Whisk is still turning add the sugar, one tablespoon at a time. The meringue should soon become stiff and should stay in the bowl even if it is turned upside-down!

❖ Spoon the meringue onto the baking parchment to form a round nest about 20cm (8") in diameter.

❖ Bake in the oven for 2 hours. If the top starts colouring too much place some greaseproof paper over the meringue. Switch off the oven and leave the meringue inside to cool.

❖ When ready to serve, use the Whisk to whip the cream to soft peaks, adding the liqueur at the end. Peel off the baking parchment and place the meringue on a serving plate.

❖ Spoon the cream into the nest and top with the fruits. Dust with a little icing sugar just before serving.

4 egg whites

pinch of salt

5ml (1 tsp) lemon juice

225g (8oz, 1 cup) caster sugar

300 ml (½ pint, 1¼ cups) double cream

15ml (1 tbsp) Amaretto di Saronno, almond liqueur

450g (1lb) fresh soft fruits such as strawberries, raspberries or pineapple, chopped into pieces

15ml (1 tbsp) icing sugar, for dusting

baking parchment cut to a circle of about 26cm (10") in diameter

☐ Oven Temperature 150°C (300°F, gas mark 2)

◯ Serves 6-8

✗ Not suitable for freezing

WHITE CHOCOLATE MOUSSE

Loved by children and adults alike. Made in advance this luxurious mousse is perfect for a dinner party - just forget about the waistline for a few minutes!

❖ Melt the chocolate in a bowl over some barely simmering water. When it has melted, whisk in the milk until smooth and leave on one side to cool.

❖ In the Kenwood Bowl whisk the egg whites with the lemon juice until they become stiff, then very gently fold into the chocolate mixture.

❖ Whisk the double cream until it just starts to form soft peaks, then fold into the chocolate mixture.

❖ Divide the mousse between four stemmed glasses and cover with plastic film. Chill for at least 2 hours, then remove plastic film and serve.

175g (6oz) good quality white chocolate, broken into small pieces

85ml (3fl oz, ⅓ cup) milk

2 egg whites

1.25ml (¼ tsp) lemon juice

225ml (8fl oz, 1 cup) double cream

✪ Serves 4

✗ Not suitable for freezing

PASSION CAKE

If you have never eaten Passion Cake before, perhaps because you don't like the sound of carrots in a cake, just try this one. Apart from being quite delicious it is not so hard on the waistline and, being made from such wholesome ingredients, is also healthy.

100g (4oz, ⅖ cup) brown sugar

2 eggs, at room temperature

85ml (3fl oz, ⅓ cup) vegetable oil

100g (4oz, 1 cup) wholemeal self raising flour

175g (6oz) carrots

1 banana, mashed

5ml (1 tsp) cinnamon

2.5ml (½ tsp) nutmeg, grated

50g (2oz, ⅔ cup) desiccated coconut

50g (2oz, ⅓ cup) raisins

☐ *Oven Temperature 180°C (350°F, gas mark 4)*

○ *Makes 1 cake - enough for 6-8 people*

✳ *Freezes well, wrapped in plastic film*

❖ Preheat the oven, then oil and line a 19cm x 9cm (7½" x 3½") loaf tin. You need only line the base.

❖ Have all the ingredients ready and weighed as this cake is quite quick to make. Grate the carrots finely.

❖ Place the sugar and eggs in the Kenwood Bowl and whisk at speed 5 for about 1 minute until they are thick and creamy.

❖ Now put the oil into a pouring jug and drizzle it into the bowl while the Whisk is still turning.

❖ Remove the Whisk and, with the Spatula, fold in the remaining ingredients. Empty the mixture into the loaf tin and bake on the middle shelf of the oven for 55 minutes until an inserted skewer comes out clean. Cool in the tin.

❖ Once cool you can split the cake in half and fill with Tangy Icing. However, make sure you also try it without icing – the cake is delicious on its own!

❖ For a nuttier variation you can add 50g (2oz) pistachio nuts to the basic mixture.

TANGY ICING

5ml (1 tsp) lemon juice

175g (6oz, ⅔ cup) cream cheese

175g (6oz, 1⅓ cups) icing sugar, sifted

zest of 1 orange, grated

○ *Makes enough to cover 1 medium-sized cake*

✗ *Not suitable for freezing*

❖ Put all the ingredients into the Kenwood Bowl and, using the K Beater at minimum speed, mix until it becomes a smooth icing.

❖ Use to fill the Passion Cake, or any other type of cake or biscuit of your own choice.

Clockwise, from
top left:

*Almond Pavlova with
Summer Fruits*

*White Chocolate
Mousse*

*Home-made Salted and
Herb Butter*

*Cajun Style Hot Crab
Soufflé*

Passion Cake

*Chicken & Leek Stuffed
Pancakes*

Olive Oil Mayonnaise

Curried Mayonnaise

KENWOOD

CHEF ❖ MAJOR

THE
TOTAL
FOOD PREPARATION
CENTRE

BLENDING - FOR SAUCES, SOUPS & SHAKES

The Liquidiser, otherwise known as a Blender when it is a free standing unit, has extremely sharp stainless steel blades which rotate at a very high speed. Food placed inside the goblet is forced to move around and across the sharp blades and is chopped finely until it becomes smooth in texture. Before the Liquidiser was introduced to the kitchen, sieving was really the only method of achieving a smooth food, but the advent of this new attachment brought a new dimension to cooking.

If I only ever made the Banana Thickshake it would be worth possessing the Liquidiser attachment. However, the list of recipes that call for this function is endless - fruit cocktails, creamy soups, smooth sauces, fresh breadcrumbs and great pâtés become so easy. Who could imagine that with a handful of ice, some coffee, icing sugar and precisely 2 minutes you could make a thick coffee mousse perfect for any dinner party dessert? Wastage becomes a thing of the past when you have a Liquidiser - any left-overs can be used to make soups, pâtés and baby food.

There are four main Liquidisers in the range - my favourite is the beautiful bold stainless steel version. It is is so unique - stainless steel always looks great and has the added bonus of keeping ingredients cool which is fantastic for cocktails. It is large and will blend up to 1.5 litres (2½ pints).

The glass Liquidiser holds 1.2 litres (2 pints) and is excellent for being able to see exactly what is going on inside. Being glass it is also scratch-resistant and especially good when using sugar.

The acrylic version makes a light and easy-to-handle Liquidiser. It is heatproof, as are all the Liquidisers, and holds 1.2 litres (2 pints).

HINTS & TIPS

❖ All the Liquidisers have a removable base which makes them easier to clean, but make sure the base is tightened before using to prevent leakage.

❖ Always remove the Liquidiser from the Chef by holding the base - never be tempted to rotate it by the handle or else you'll lose the whole preparation!

❖ It is often better to blend the food in batches rather than to overfill the goblet.

❖ The Liquidisers are all safe for use with hot liquids but it is better to allow food to cool a little before blending for added security.

Soups

Celeriac & Blue Cheese Soup

❖ Peel the celeriac and cut into 1 cm (½") cubes. Put into a bowl of water with the lemon juice.

❖ Melt the butter in a saucepan over a low heat and add the potato and onion. Sauté gently for 3-4 minutes then drain the celeriac, discarding the juice, and add to the pan. Cook for a further 5 minutes.

❖ Add the stock and simmer gently for 30 minutes, until the vegetables are soft. Remove the pan from the heat and stir in the cheese and cream.

❖ Blend at minimum speed until the soup is smooth. Reheat gently just before serving.

250g (9oz) celeriac, weighed after peeling

15ml (1 tbsp) lemon juice

25g (1oz, ⅛ cup) butter

1 medium potato, peeled and chopped

½ small onion, peeled and sliced

575ml (1 pint, 2¼ cups) chicken or vegetable stock

75g (3oz, ⅔ cup) blue cheese, chopped with rind removed

75ml (2½ fl oz, ¼ cup) double cream

✪ *Serves 4*

✗ *Not suitable for freezing*

Fisherman's Shrimp Bisque

❖ Heat the oil in a heavy-based pan and gently sauté the potatoes, onion, tomatoes and garlic for 10 minutes.

❖ Add the stock, milk and prawns and bring to the boil. Cover and simmer gently for 20 minutes.

❖ Cool slightly before blending in batches until the soup is smooth.

❖ Season to taste with salt and black pepper, return the soup to the pan, then reheat gently and serve with plenty of bread.

30ml (2 tbsp) oil

2 medium potatoes, peeled and chopped

1 onion, peeled and chopped

2 tomatoes, halved

2 cloves garlic, peeled and chopped

575ml (1 pint, 2¼ cups) chicken or vegetable stock

300ml (½ pint, 1¼ cups) milk

225g (8oz, 2 cups) fresh or frozen prawns or shrimps, shelled

salt and freshly milled black pepper

✪ *Serves 4*

✗ *Not suitable for freezing*

INSTANT SPRING VEGETABLE SOUP

2 medium potatoes, cooked, or 175g (6oz) canned potatoes or flageolet beans

1 carrot, cleaned

1 leek, white and light green part only, cleaned and cut into 2cm (1") pieces

1 stick celery, cut into 2cm (1") pieces

1 fresh tomato

1 stock cube, either vegetable, chicken or beef

575ml (1 pint, 2¼ cups) freshly boiled water

salt and freshly milled black pepper

✿ *Serves 4*

✗ *Not suitable for freezing*

❖ Place the vegetables in the Liquidiser and sprinkle over the stock cube.

❖ Allow the boiled water to cool for 2 minutes then pour into the Liquidiser to cover the vegetables.

❖ Blend at minimum speed for 2-4 minutes, then season to taste with salt and black pepper.

❖ Serve immediately for a quick snack with chunks of fresh bread.

BORTSCH

A popular Russian soup characterised by its beetroot-red colour.

1 medium onion

1 small potato

225g (8oz) raw beetroot

575ml (1 pint, 2¼ cups) vegetable stock

15ml (1 tbsp) white wine vinegar

2.5ml (½ tsp) yeast extract

salt and freshly milled black pepper

90ml (6 tbsp) Greek-style yoghurt, for garnishing

✿ *Serves 6*

✗ *Not suitable for freezing*

❖ Peel and roughly chop the onion, potato and beetroot before placing in a large saucepan.

❖ Add the vegetable stock and simmer, covered, for about 50 minutes until the beetroot is soft.

❖ Cool, then blend in batches until the soup is smooth.

❖ When ready to serve reheat, gently adding the vinegar and yeast extract.

❖ Season to taste with salt and black pepper then pour into bowls and decorate with a spoonful of Greek-style yoghurt.

GAZPACHO

Quick and simple, this soup captures the very essence of summer. Serve it chilled on a hot day with some croûtons, and possibly an ice cube in each bowl to enhance the icy nature of the soup.

❖ Firstly skin the tomatoes by pouring boiling water over them and leaving for 2 minutes. Remove from the water and, when cool enough to handle, remove the skins.

❖ Place the tomatoes in the Liquidiser with the garlic and herbs and blend until smooth.

❖ Pour into a bowl then stir in the rest of the ingredients. Season to taste with salt, black pepper and cayenne pepper. Chill for 30 minutes in a freezer or 2 hours in a refrigerator. The soup must be well chilled.

❖ Just before serving, taste for seasoning again as chilling will reduce the strength of the flavours.

❖ Float an ice cube in each bowl and sprinkle over the croûtons if desired. If it is a chilly day this soup is just as delicious served hot.

450g (1lb) tomatoes, ripened

1 clove garlic, peeled

30ml (2 tbsp) fresh herbs such as basil and parsley

2 spring onions, finely chopped

½ green pepper, deseeded and very finely chopped

5cm (2") piece cucumber, very finely chopped

15ml (1 tbsp) lemon juice

15ml (1 tbsp) tomato juice or 2.5ml (½ tsp) tomato purée

30ml (2 tbsp) olive oil

salt, black pepper and cayenne pepper

4 ice cubes and croûtons, for serving, optional

✪ *Serves 6*
✗ *Not suitable for freezing*

Sauces

Mediterranean Tomato Sauce

The smoky flavours of charred tomatoes are really captured in this lively tomato sauce. Adorable with pasta, burgers or fish.

450g (1lb) plum tomatoes, ripened
2 cloves garlic, peeled
30ml (2 tbsp) olive oil
15 basil leaves
salt and freshly ground black pepper

○ *Makes enough sauce for 2 servings*
✗ *Not suitable for freezing*

❖ Place the tomatoes in boiling water for 2 minutes. Drain and, when cool enough, remove the skins. Slice in half and place in a bowl.

❖ Slice the garlic cloves in half lengthways. Add these to the bowl along with the olive oil and basil then season with salt and black pepper. Stir well to coat the tomatoes, garlic and basil in the olive oil, then tip into a large, heavy-based frying pan.

❖ Turn the tomato halves so that the cut side is facing uppermost. Set the pan over a medium heat until you can just hear a sizzling sound then leave, uncovered, for 30 minutes. By now the tomatoes should have shrunk a little in size and be charred underneath.

❖ Allow to cool a little then pour into the Liquidiser, ensuring that you scrape all the charred bits from the bottom of the pan. Blend until smooth and serve with pasta or Herb Butter Beefburgers.

Smoked Salmon Tagliatelle with Red Pepper Sauce

2 red peppers
150ml (¼ pint, ½ cup) white wine
1 chicken stock cube
250ml (9oz, 1¼ cups) crème fraîche
325g (12oz) tagliatelle
100g (4oz) smoked salmon, thinly sliced
salt, for cooking

❂ *Serves 4*
✗ *Not suitable for freezing*

❖ Firstly make the sauce by halving the red peppers and removing the stalks and seeds. Grill at the highest setting, skin side uppermost, until the skin is completely charred and blackened.

❖ Meanwhile, boil the white wine until it has reduced by half the quantity and leave to cool for a short while. Allow the peppers to cool then remove the skins.

❖ Blend 3 of the pepper halves with the white wine in the Liquidiser and pour the mixture back into the pan. Slice the remaining pepper half very thinly into Julienne strips and add to the pan with the stock cube.

❖ Simmer gently for 5 minutes. Reduce the heat and stir in the crème fraîche.

❖ Bring a large pan of water to the boil, add a good helping of salt, then carefully place in the tagliatelle and simmer until 'al dente'. Drain, then stir in the smoked salmon and sauce. Serve immediately.

PÂTÉS & TOPPINGS

CHICKEN LIVER PÂTÉ WITH GREEN OLIVES

This smooth velvety pâté makes a perfect first course as it requires no last minute attention.

❖ Heat half the butter in a pan over a low heat. Sauté the onion and garlic very gently in the butter for 5 minutes until soft but not coloured.

❖ Add the chicken livers and sauté for 5 minutes on either side so that they are cooked but still slightly pink on the inside.

❖ Remove from the heat and stir in the rest of the butter, green olives and brandy.

❖ When the butter has melted, tip the contents of the pan into the Liquidiser, season generously with salt and black pepper then blend for 2 minutes until smooth.

❖ Stop the Liquidiser and taste for seasoning – the flavour is lessened by the chilling so make sure it is well seasoned.

❖ Pour into a terracotta dish or pâté dish, cover and refrigerate for at least 12 hours. Serve with toast.

225g (8oz, 1 cup) butter
1 large onion, finely chopped
2 cloves garlic, peeled and crushed
450g (1lb) chicken livers, fresh or frozen and thoroughly defrosted
30 green olives, pitted
salt and freshly milled black pepper
30ml (2 tbsp) brandy

✿ *Serves 8*
✗ *Not suitable for freezing*

AVOCADO MOUSSE PÂTÉ

❖ Cut the avocados in half, peel and remove the stone.

❖ Place them in the Liquidiser with the stock, lemon juice, garlic, crème fraîche and mayonnaise.

❖ Blend until smooth before pouring into individual serving dishes. Cover and refrigerate for a few hours then serve with toast either as a first course or as a lunch pâté.

2 avocados, ripened
150ml (¼ pint, ½ cup) chicken or vegetable stock, cooled
juice of half a lemon
1 clove garlic, peeled and chopped
150ml (¼ pint, ½ cup) crème fraîche
150ml (¼ pint, ½ cup) mayonnaise

✿ *Serves 6-8 as a first course or lunch pâté*
✗ *Not suitable for freezing*

LAMB TOPPED WITH A HERB CRUST

The Liquidiser makes breadcrumbs in no time and is useful for a recipe such as this which uses a breadcrumb topping.

25g (1oz, ⅛ cup) butter

60ml (4 tbsp) mixed fresh herbs, such as parsley, dill, basil, chives

50g (2oz, 1 packed cup) fresh white bread, crusts removed

325-450g (12-16oz) rack of lamb (6 ribs), excess fat removed

salt and freshly milled black pepper

☐ *Oven Temperature 190°C (375°F, gas mark 5)*

✪ *Serves 2*

✗ *Not suitable for freezing*

❖ Preheat the oven. Gently melt the butter and finely chop the herbs.

❖ Make the breadcrumbs in batches in the liquidiser, emptying the crumbs into a bowl as you go. Mix the breadcrumbs, chopped herbs and melted butter together and season generously with salt and black pepper.

❖ Place the rack of lamb on a baking sheet and pack the crumb mixture on to the top side from which most of the fat should have been removed.

❖ Bake for 35 minutes if you like your lamb to be pink, or 45 minutes if you prefer it to be well done.

❖ Serve in individual rib slices.

PEANUT ROAST

1 medium onion

25g (1oz, ⅛ cup) butter

225g (8oz, 1½ cups) peanuts

100g (4oz, 3⅓ cups) wholemeal bread, crusts removed

300ml (½ pint, 1¼ cups) vegetable stock

10ml (2 tsp) yeast extract

5ml (1 tsp) mixed herbs

freshly milled black pepper

50g (2oz, ⅔ cup) cheese, grated

1 tomato

loaf tin with base measurements 9cm x 19cm (3½" x 7½") lined with greaseproof paper

☐ *Oven Temperature 180°C (350°F, gas mark 4)*

✪ *Serves 6*

✗ *Not suitable for freezing*

❖ Preheat the oven. Peel and dice the onion and sauté, in the butter, over a fairly low heat for 20-30 minutes until golden brown.

❖ Meanwhile, prepare the rest of the ingredients. If the peanuts are ready-salted, tip them into a sieve and shake over the sink to remove the salt.

❖ Make the breadcrumbs and chop the nuts at the same time in batches in the Liquidiser. The bread should be crumb-like but still retain a little texture.

❖ When the onions have turned golden pour in the vegetable stock then stir in the yeast extract and herbs. Bring to simmering point, remove from the heat then stir in the nuts and breadcrumbs. Season to taste with black pepper.

❖ Press half the mixture into the prepared loaf tin and sprinkle with the grated cheese. Slice the tomato and place in a single layer over the cheese before pressing in the remaining mixture over the top of the tomato.

❖ Bake for 45 minutes until the top is nicely browned. Cool slightly in the tin before turning onto a plate for serving. Nut roast is also delicious served cold as a pâté.

DRINKS, SHAKES & COCKTAILS

KENWOOD LEMONADE

This lemonade recipe was created by Kenwood many years ago to demonstrate the sharpness of the stainless steel blades. Today, Kenwood Lemonade is still demonstrated in many countries of the world and has never yet failed to catch the crowd's attention.

The ice makes it cool and refreshing while the egg gives it a frothy, almost fizzy, texture. Plenty of calcium makes it a nourishing, fun drink for the children. Try stirring in some gin for an after-sunset cocktail when the children have gone to bed!

❖ Place the ice cubes, sugar, lemon and whole egg, still in its shell, in the Liquidiser. Add the water and put on the lid.

❖ Blend at maximum speed for 10–20 seconds.

❖ Strain through a sieve, into a jug, and serve with extra ice cubes and lemon slices floating on the top, for decoration.

1 lemon, thin-skinned variety, washed

30ml (2 tbsp) sugar

100g (4oz) ice cubes or 6 large cubes

575ml (1 pint, 2¼ cups) water, chilled

1 whole egg, in the shell, washed

✿ *Serves 4-6*
✗ *Not suitable for freezing*

EXOTIC FRUIT COCKTAIL

❖ Skin the mango and paw paw or papaya and remove the pips.

❖ Place in the Liquidiser with the remaining ingredients, and blend at a high speed until thick and smooth. Serve immediately.

½ mango

½ paw paw or papaya

300ml (½ pint, 1¼ cups) natural yoghurt

30ml (2 tbsp) honey

15ml (1 tbsp) lemon juice

✿ *Serves 2*
✗ *Not suitable for freezing*

BANANA THICKSHAKE

One spectacularly hot afternoon recently, a few Liquidiser-happy friends who came for a weekend by the sea meant we thick-shaked our way through 3 tubs of ice cream and a couple of bunches of bananas. Even after all that, we still think this yummy drink is our favourite.

2 bananas
200ml (7fl oz, ¾ cup) milk
5ml (1 tsp) vanilla essence
6 scoops (each about the size of an egg) vanilla ice cream

○ *Makes 2 large glasses*
✗ *Not suitable for freezing*

❖ Put all the ingredients into the Liquidiser and blend at speed 1 to 2 until smooth. Serve immediately.

CAFÉ LIÉGOIS (INSTANT COFFEE SORBET)

Though it is made with just ice, sugar and coffee, the resulting texture of this dessert is miraculously thick and creamy, almost like milkshake.

It can be made from start to finish in just 2 minutes and is simple providing you follow the recipe exactly. Try it a couple of times before showing it off to guests as it needs a little practice at first.

225g (8oz) ice cubes or 12 large cubes
105ml (7 tbsp) water
30ml (2 tbsp) instant coffee, granules or powder
90ml (6 tbsp) icing sugar
wafer biscuits and whipped cream, for serving

✪ *Serves 4*
✗ *Not suitable for freezing*

❖ Make sure you follow this recipe, carefully adding the ingredients to the Liquidiser in the given order. Also, have the measured icing sugar ready at hand.

❖ Put the ice into the goblet followed by the water and lastly the instant coffee. Blend at minimum speed for 45 seconds.

❖ Increase the speed to 1 for 15 seconds. During the 15 seconds remove the lid cap.

❖ Increase the speed to 3 and add the icing sugar, a spoonful at a time. This should take no more than 10 seconds.

❖ Turn the speed to maximum and blend for 5 seconds. You should now have a thick mousse-like dessert which can be spooned into glasses for serving straight away. If not then try it again, it is well worth the effort!

Clockwise, from
top left:

Exotic Fruit Cocktail

Café Liégois

*Smoked Salmon
Tagliatelle with Red
Pepper Sauce*

Kenwood Lemonade

*Fisherman's Shrimp
Bisque*

Bortsch

*Chicken Liver Pâté
with Green Olives*

*Mediterranean Tomato
Sauce*

*Celeriac & Blue Cheese
Soup*

Avocado Mousse Pâté

Gazpacho

Mincing at Home - the secret of Successful Minced Dishes

We are a world that loves mince and whichever country you may choose to visit you can be certain that it has its own unique way of using this popular ingredient. Countless delicious and tempting recipes are proof of the enormous versatility and inspiration that mince offers both the creative cook and the busy family.

With the Mincer attachment you are not confined to just beef or lamb - you can also choose chicken, fish, duck and rabbit as well as vegetables. Children seem to adore mince, be it in the form of fish fingers or hamburgers, just as much as adults love Lasagne or Chilli con Carne. These are Western favourites, so what about the East? The Chinese carefully spice their mince then they wrap it in pastry and either deep-fry or steam it to make wanton or dumplings. In India they make lamb koftas, which are spiced and then fried.

Whatever use you have for mince, dishes are more satisfying when you prepare the mince yourself. This is because of the versatility that it allows you, and because you can be sure of the quality of the final mince, but most of all because recipes taste far superior when you use your own home-made mince.

Two sizes of Mincer enable you to choose according to your needs. Both have a coarse and a fine screen for varying the texture of the mince and the larger No. 8 mincer also has stainless steel components inside to guard against corrosion.

Once you possess the Mincer you can make many other things by using any one of the adaptors that have been designed to fit the attachment. Choose from sausages, Middle Eastern Kebbe, cookies and fine grating and transform your Mincer into a versatile attachment.

Hints & Tips

❖ Put a piece of bread into the tube at the end of mincing to help push out any remaining meat.

❖ Make cleaning more simple by using the brush provided.

❖ The larger No. 8 version comes with a lid. Turn this over and you can also use it to collect the mince as it is extruded. Keep your Sausage Maker or Kebbe Maker adaptor and extra screens inside the specially-designed pusher.

❖ Use the Mincer between speeds 4 and maximum.

HERB BUTTER BEEFBURGERS

Huge and juicy, these beefburgers are hard to beat.

❖ Use the K Beater at minimum speed to beat the herbs into the butter. Now wrap the herb butter in plastic film, roll into a fat sausage shape, about 5cm (2") in length and leave in the freezer to harden while you mince the meat.

❖ Cut the beef into long, thin pieces and feed it into the tube of the Mincer. When you have minced the meat, pass it back through a second time as this makes the texture of the beefburger really superb.

❖ Now add the lemon juice and zest, then season well with black pepper, (do not add salt as this draws out the juices) and, using the K Beater at minimum speed, mix it all together.

❖ Divide the mixture into 4 equally-sized balls. Unwrap the hardened butter roll and slice it widthways into 4 evenly-sized pieces. Press one slice into the centre of each meat ball and shape into 4cm (1½") thick burgers.

❖ Cover with plastic film and refrigerate until ready to use.

❖ To cook, firstly season well with salt. Place under the grill, preheated to the highest setting, and cook for 4 minutes on each side, or barbecue for the same amount of time.

❖ Herb Butter Beefburgers taste really good served with rice, a crisp salad and Mediterranean Tomato Sauce (see page 52).

30ml (2 tbsp) mixed fresh herbs, such as basil, parsley, thyme, finely chopped

50g (2oz, ¼ cup) butter, at room temperature

675g (1½ lb) beef, sirloin or braising steak is suitable

juice of half a lemon

zest of half a lemon, grated

freshly milled black pepper

salt

○ *Makes 4 beefburgers*

✳ *Suitable for freezing - make sure they are well defrosted before using*

Kashmiri Koftas in Flaked Almonds with Spicy Yoghurt Sauce

Kofta Balls:

450g (1 lb) lean lamb

5ml (1 tsp) fresh ginger, grated

1 fresh green chilli, seeds removed, chopped finely

5ml (1 tsp) ground coriander

5ml (1 tsp) curry powder

1.25ml (¼ tsp) chilli powder

5ml (1 tsp) salt

15ml (1 tbsp) plain yoghurt

10ml (2 tsp) dried milk powder

85g (3oz, 1 cup) flaked almonds

Sauce:

150g (5oz, ⅔ cup) plain yoghurt

15ml (1 tbsp) dried milk powder

5ml (1 tsp) sugar

2.5ml (½ tsp) salt

15ml (1 tbsp) salad oil

☐ *Oven Temperature 190°C (375°F, gas mark 5)*

○ *Makes 12 balls - enough for 4 servings*

✗ *Not suitable for freezing*

❖ Preheat the oven. Cut the lamb into strips, discarding any fatty bits, and then mince, using the fine mincing screen, into the Kenwood Bowl.

❖ Mix the lamb with the ginger, chilli, coriander, curry powder, chilli powder, salt, yoghurt and milk powder, using the K Beater at minimum speed.

❖ When the mixture is well combined, divide into 12 balls each of about 5cm (2") in diameter.

❖ Roll the balls in the flaked almonds and place in a baking tray leaving sufficient space in between each one for them to expand during cooking.

❖ Stir together the sauce ingredients and spoon the mixture over the top of the kofta balls making sure each one is well coated.

❖ Bake uncovered for 30 minutes, by which time the flaked almonds should be nicely toasted. These are delicious when served with an Indian-style rice salad.

AMERICAN MEATLOAF WITH ONION GRAVY

- ❖ Preheat the oven. Cut the beef into strips then mince, using the coarse screen, into the Kenwood Bowl.
- ❖ If you are using fresh herbs chop them finely. Add them to the bowl with the Worcestershire sauce, basil, parsley, paprika, salt, chilli sauce, and some freshly milled black pepper. Using the K Beater at minimum speed, mix all the ingredients together.
- ❖ Oil a bread tin with base measurements 9cm x 19cm (3½" x 7½")
- ❖ Press the mixture into the bread tin and bake for 1 hour. Allow to cool, then pour off the juices.
- ❖ Roll out the Puff Pastry to a rectangle 38cm x 36cm (15" x 14½") and place the meatloaf lengthways in the middle. Cut out a square from each corner of the pastry up to about 1cm (½") from the edge of the meatloaf. Save these corners to make pastry leaves.
- ❖ Brush each edge of the pastry with the beaten egg. Coat the top and sides of the meatloaf with the tomato ketchup and bring the two pastry ends up and over the top of the loaf.
- ❖ Brush the top of the pastry with the egg then bring one of the pastry sides up and over so that the corners of the meatloaf are sealed well. Brush the top again with the egg and bring the remaining pastry side up to meet it, allowing it to overlap a little.
- ❖ Cut out 2 or 3 pastry leaves from the remaining pastry pieces and lay them on top to decorate. Brush the complete loaf with the remaining egg and place on a baking sheet.
- ❖ Bake for 30 minutes until golden and serve, in slices, with the Onion Gravy.
- ❖ To make the Onion Gravy, heat the oil in a heavy-based pan over quite a gentle heat.
- ❖ Sauté the onions in the oil, stirring occasionally for at least 30 minutes until they are a rich brown colour, but not burnt. It is very important to let the colour develop slowly as this is how the gravy obtains its distinctive flavour.
- ❖ Stir in the flour and let it fry for 2 minutes. Add the stock and the Meatloaf juices, stirring vigorously until it comes to the boil and thickens. Stir in the soy sauce and oyster sauce then season to taste with salt and black pepper.

MEATLOAF:

900g (2 lb) stewing steak

10ml (2 tsp) Worcestershire sauce

30ml (2 tbsp) fresh basil or 10ml (2 tsp) dried basil

30ml (2 tbsp) fresh parsley or 10ml (2 tsp) dried parsley

15ml (3 tsp) paprika

10ml (2 tsp) salt

10ml (2 tsp) hot chilli sauce

freshly milled black pepper

1 quantity, 250g (9oz) Puff Pastry, (see p.20)

1 egg, for glazing

30ml (2 tbsp) tomato ketchup

ONION GRAVY:

30ml (2 tbsp) oil

2 large onions, peeled and thinly sliced

22.5ml (1½ tbsp) flour

425g (¾ pint, 1¾ cups) beef stock

left-over juices from the baked Meatloaf

5ml (1 tsp) soy sauce

5ml (1 tsp) oyster sauce, optional

salt and freshly milled black pepper

☐ *Oven Temperature 180°C (350°F, gas mark 4)*

✺ *Serves 6-8*

✳ *Suitable for freezing before baking, defrost for at least 6 hours beforehand*

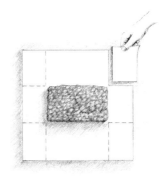

CRISPY DUCK PARCELS WITH ORANGE SAUCE

Chinese-style duck in crispy filo parcels with a tangy orange sauce make this first course a firm favourite.

DUCK PARCELS:

175g (6oz) duck, skin and bones removed

2.5ml (½ tsp) Chinese five spice powder

1 clove garlic, peeled and crushed

2.5ml (½ tsp) fresh ginger, finely grated

5ml (1 tsp) sesame oil

2.5ml (½ tsp) salt

2 spring onions, finely chopped

8 square sheets filo pastry measuring 15cm x 15cm (6"x 6")

10g (½ oz) melted butter, for brushing

ORANGE SAUCE:

5ml (1 tsp) butter

5ml (1 tsp) sugar

150ml (¼ pint, ½ cup) orange juice

1 chicken stock cube, dissolved in 150ml (¼ pint, ½ cup) hot water

5ml (1 tsp) soy sauce

5ml (1 tsp) cornflour dissolved in 15ml (1 tbsp) cold water

2 pieces Chinese stem ginger in syrup, cut into small pieces, optional

salt and freshly milled black pepper

☐ *Oven Temperature 180°C (350°F, gas mark 4)*

✪ *Serves 4 as a first course*

✗ *Not suitable for freezing*

❖ Preheat the oven. Make the duck parcels by firstly mincing the duck, using the fine screen, straight into the Kenwood Bowl.

❖ Add the Chinese five spice powder, garlic, ginger, sesame oil, salt and spring onions, then mix together using the K Beater at minimum speed.

❖ Lay out separately 4 square sheets of filo pastry and brush each with a little melted butter.

❖ Place another sheet, at an angle, on top of each square so that it forms an 8-point star shape.

❖ Place a quarter of the duck mixture on to the middle of each filo pastry star.

❖ Brush the exposed pastry with butter then bring up the pastry edges to make a small bag, pinching tightly together to seal.

❖ Brush the outsides of the parcels with butter and bake for 25 minutes until golden brown.

❖ Meanwhile make the sauce by first melting the butter in a small, heavy-based pan. Add the sugar to the butter and fry until it caramelises.

❖ Add the orange juice, stock and soy sauce then simmer for 5 minutes. Pour in the cornflour mixture, stirring constantly until the sauce has thickened.

❖ Add the ginger, if being used, and season to taste with salt and black pepper. Keep the sauce warm until the duck parcels are cooked.

❖ To serve, pour a little sauce on to 4 warm plates, place a duck parcel in the middle of each and drizzle more sauce over the top.

Cajun Style Chicken Meatballs

Hot and spicy, these chicken balls are cooked with soured cream and red peppers for a really delicious supper.

❖ Mince the chicken, using the fine screen, straight into the Kenwood Bowl.

❖ Use the K Beater at minimum speed to mix in the Cajun spices, chilli sauce, salt, parsley and cornflour.

❖ Divide the mixture into 12, roll into balls and coat each ball in the flour to make it less sticky.

❖ To cook, heat the oil in a pan over a medium heat and add the chicken balls. Shallow fry for 10 minutes, turning occasionally until they are nicely browned.

❖ Meanwhile, slice the pepper into thin strips. Add the strips to the pan and turn the heat to high.

❖ Fry the chicken balls for a further 5 minutes until the pepper is slightly burnt at the edges.

❖ Remove from the heat, pour in the soured cream and season well with salt and black pepper. Let the cream bubble while the pan is cooling. Serve on a bed of rice with a fresh green salad.

450g (1 lb) chicken thighs, bones and skin removed

10ml (2 tsp) Cajun style spices (the ready-blended type are easiest)

10ml (2 tsp) hot chilli sauce

2.75ml (¼ tsp) salt

15ml (1 tbsp) fresh parsley, finely chopped

5ml (1 tsp) cornflour

30ml (2 tbsp) plain flour, for rolling

30ml (2 tbsp) oil, for frying

1 red pepper, deseeded

60ml (4 tbsp) soured cream

salt and freshly milled black pepper

✿ *Serves 4*

✗ *Not suitable for freezing*

Coarse Country Pâté

❖ Preheat the oven. Mince the livers, pork and kidney, using the coarse mincing screen.

❖ Cut the rinds from the bacon and, using a rolling pin, flatten the rashers to make them thinner with a larger surface area.

❖ Line an ovenproof pâté dish with the bacon, placing each rasher side by side, and leaving enough length so that the rashers can be folded over the top of the pâté.

❖ Using the K Beater at speed 1, mix the minced meats with the onion, garlic, peppercorns, sherry, egg and salt. Season to taste with black pepper.

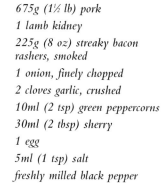

❖ Spoon the mixture into the pâté dish. Fold the bacon rashers over the top and bake, covered, for 1¼ hours. Leave to cool in the dish, then transfer to a serving plate. Serve sliced with crusty bread.

450g (1 lb) chicken livers

675g (1½ lb) pork

1 lamb kidney

225g (8 oz) streaky bacon rashers, smoked

1 onion, finely chopped

2 cloves garlic, crushed

10ml (2 tsp) green peppercorns

30ml (2 tbsp) sherry

1 egg

5ml (1 tsp) salt

freshly milled black pepper

❑ *Oven Temperature 170°C (325°F, gas mark 3)*

✿ *Serves 8-10*

✗ *Not suitable for freezing*

CHEESY FISH CAKES

Fish cakes always make a popular meal - these ones are very easy to prepare and taste really delicious.

175g (6oz, 3 packed cups) fresh white bread, crusts removed

325g (12oz) white fish such as halibut, huss, cod, skin and bones removed

15ml (1 tbsp) lemon juice

15ml (1 tbsp) cornflour

2.5ml (½ tsp) salt

1 egg

30ml (2 tbsp) crème fraîche

30ml (1 tbsp) chives, chopped

100g (4oz, 1⅓ cups) Cheddar or Emmental cheese, grated

freshly milled black pepper

a little oil, for frying

○ Makes 8

✗ Not suitable for freezing

❖ Make the breadcrumbs in batches in the Liquidiser.

❖ Mince the fish, using the fine screen, straight into the Kenwood Bowl. Add the remaining ingredients and mix together, using the K Beater at minimum speed. Season with black pepper.

❖ Divide the mixture into 8 and make each into a triangular shape. Shallow-fry the cakes over a gentle heat for 8 minutes on each side.

❖ Serve hot with fresh vegetables.

Clockwise, from
centre top:

American Meatloaf

Coarse Country Pâté

*Cajun Style Chicken
Meatballs*

Cheesy Fish Cakes

*Kashmiri Koftas in
Flaked Almonds*

Crispy Duck Parcel

Sizzling Sausages, with Endless Variations

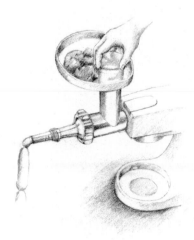

There is scarcely a country in the world which does not claim at least one distinctively national sausage, and some like France, Germany and Italy have developed sausage making into a highly specialised charcuterie. Steeped in history, the humble sausage is fast becoming the fashionable food of the nineties. Burgundy pistachio, smoked salmon, venison and chestnut, spinach and artichoke are just a few to be found in specialist sausage shops.

The Sausage Maker Adaptor is easy to use, and will give you endless hours of fun. It comes with two sizes of nozzle, one for standard sausages, the other for small cocktail sausages.

Almost any meat or combination of meats, as well as nuts, lentils, fish and seafood can be used for sausages.

Eggs and breadcrumbs are usually added to the ingredients for bulk and binding.

Casings & Coverings

Sausage casings come in two different sizes - the standard size casings are from the pig, the small casings from sheep. Your local butcher should be able to provide you with what you need. Keep the casings in a bowl of water in the refrigerator as this makes them easier to use - any that are left can be frozen in a little water. Vegetarian casings are available for vegetarian sausages, or these can be rolled and coated in ground nuts, sesame seeds or breadcrumbs.

Making Skinned Sausages

❖ Dab the end of the adaptor nozzle with a little water and slip on the skins, pushing them up the nozzle as far as possible.

❖ Form the sausage filling into walnut-sized pieces and place on the feed tray.

❖ Switch the Chef to minimum speed and start feeding the pieces of sausage filling into the Mincer. Grasp the end of the sausage casing and monitor the amount being fed into it. Sometimes the casing becomes stuck, so help slip it off the nozzle where necessary.

❖ When the casing is full and the filling has all been used, twist the casing to form individual lengths, of approximately 10cm (4") for standard or 4 cm (1½") for cocktail sausages, making sure that there is enough room in the casing so that they don't become too tight.

PORK, FENNEL & PAPRIKA SAUSAGES

The paprika gives a really authentic, Spanish flavour, the fennel a special tang. They are particularly delicious served with Mediterranean Tomato Sauce (see page 52).

❖ Fit the coarse screen on to the Mincer attachment. Cut the pork into long thin, strips and mince directly into the Kenwood Bowl. When all of the pork has been minced, feed some of it back through the Mincer - this helps to push through any remaining strips of meat. Switch off the Chef and remove the Mincer.

❖ Add the remaining ingredients to the Bowl, then mix together, using the K Beater at minimum speed.

❖ Remove any remaining meat from the Mincer, then replace the screen and cutting blade with the Sausage Maker Adaptor and assemble the attachment on the Chef. Feed the sausage mixture through the adaptor, filling the sausage casing as described on page 66.

❖ To cook the sausages, heat a little oil in a frying pan over a gentle heat. Fry slowly for at least 25 minutes, (10 minutes for cocktail size) turning occasionally, to allow all the flavours to finally develop.

450g (1lb) belly of pork, weighed after the skin and ribs have been removed

2.5ml (½ tsp) black peppercorns, coarsely crushed, not ground

2.5ml (½ tsp) dried fennel seeds

10ml (2 tsp) salt

freshly milled black pepper

15ml (3 tsp) paprika

1 egg

25g (1oz, ½ packed cup) fresh breadcrumbs

length of sausage casing, standard or small depending on size of sausage desired

oil, for cooking

❍ *Makes 8 standard or 32 cocktail sausages*

✳ *Suitable for freezing*

LAMB, ROSEMARY & LEMON SAUSAGES

❖ Fit the coarse screen on to the Mincer attachment and mince the lamb directly into the Kenwood Bowl. Pass the minced lamb through the attachment a second time, before switching off the Chef and removing the Mincer.

❖ Add the remaining ingredients to the lamb and combine thoroughly using the K Beater at minimum speed.

❖ Remove any remaining meat from the Mincer, then replace the screen and cutting blade with the Sausage Maker Adaptor and assemble the attachment on the Chef.

❖ Feed the mixture through the adaptor, filling the sausage casing as described on page 66.

❖ These sausages are particularly succulent when barbecued, but taste equally as good fried or grilled. Barbecue for approximately 15 minutes for standard size, 5 minutes for cocktail size.

775g (1¼ lb) lamb, preferably shoulder, bones removed

100g (4oz, 2 packed cups) fresh breadcrumbs

2 cloves garlic

7.75ml (1¼ tsp) salt

10ml (2 tsp) dried rosemary

freshly milled black pepper

2 eggs

15ml (1 tbsp) lemon juice

length of sausage casing, standard or small depending on size of sausage desired

❍ *Makes 16 standard or 60 cocktail sausages*

✳ *Suitable for freezing*

CHINESE CHICKEN SAUSAGES

FILLING:

450g (1lb) chicken thighs, weighed after the skin and bones have been removed

2.5ml (½ tsp) Chinese five spice powder

30ml (2 tbsp) light soy sauce

15ml (1 tbsp) chives, finely chopped

2.5ml (½ tsp) sugar

2.5ml (½ tsp) salt

5ml (1 tsp) fresh ginger, finely grated

1 clove garlic, crushed

10ml (2 tsp) cornflour

10ml (2 tsp) sesame oil

7.5ml (1½ tsp) barbecue or plum sauce

COATING - SKINNED SAUSAGES:

length of sausage casing, standard or small depending on size of sausage desired

COATING - SKINLESS SAUSAGES:

15ml (1 tbsp) flour and 15ml (1 tbsp) sesame seeds

oil, for cooking

○ Makes 8 skinned or skinless standard sausages or 32 skinned cocktail sausages

✳ Suitable for freezing

❖ Fit the fine screen on to the Mincer attachment and mince the chicken directly into the Kenwood Bowl. Switch off the Chef and remove the Mincer.

❖ Add the remaining ingredients to the Bowl and mix together using the K Beater at minimum speed.

❖ Remove any remaining meat from the Mincer, then replace the screen and cutting blade with the Sausage Maker Adaptor and assemble the attachment on the Chef.

❖ If you're making skinned sausages, fill the casing using the method as described on page 66.

❖ If you want to leave them skinless, sprinkle the flour and sesame seeds on to a large tray, then as the sausage meat leaves the adaptor, lay it on the tray so that the sausage lies in a straight line from one end to the other.

❖ When the sausage reaches the end of the tray, switch off the Chef, and cut off the sausage length.

❖ Roll the sausage over to cover it well in the mixed flour and sesame seeds.

❖ Cut into suitable lengths and transfer the individual sausages to a separate floured plate.

❖ Repeat this process until all the filling has been used. Don't forget to push through the last of the filling with some bread pieces which have been soaked in a little water and squeezed to remove any excess.

❖ Heat a little oil in a frying pan then cook the skinless sausages over a gentle heat for 10 minutes. Turn them over and cook for 10 minutes more. For skinned sausages cook slowly for 25 minutes in a frying pan (10 minutes for cocktail, size) or 15 minutes on a barbecue (5 minutes for cocktail size).

SMOKED SALMON SAUSAGES

❖ Fit the fine screen on to the Mincer attachment, then mince the salmon tail and smoked salmon directly into the Kenwood Bowl. Switch off the Chef and remove the Mincer.

❖ Add the remaining ingredients to the Bowl. Mix together using the K Beater at minimum speed.

❖ Cover and refrigerate the mixture for at least 2 hours to make it cooler and therefore easier to work with.

❖ Remove any remaining fish from the Mincer, then replace the screen and cutting blade with the Sausage Maker Adaptor and assemble the attachment on the Chef.

❖ Feed the mixture through the adaptor, then cut to convenient lengths. Fry the sausages gently in butter to cook. These are delicious served with a fresh salad.

175g (6oz) salmon tail, skin and bones removed

50g (2oz) smoked salmon, the off-cuts are ideal for this recipe

225g (8oz, 4 packed cups) fresh white breadcrumbs

15ml (1 tbsp) lemon juice

30ml (2 tbsp) crème fraîche

45ml (3 tbsp) fresh chives, finely chopped

1 egg

5ml (1 tsp) salt

freshly milled black pepper

butter, for frying

○ *Makes 16 standard sausages*
✗ *Not suitable for freezing*

NUTTY VEGETARIAN SAUSAGES

❖ Fry the onion in the oil for about 10 minutes until golden.

❖ Place all the ingredients, including the fried onion, into the Kenwood Bowl and mix together using the K Beater at minimum speed.

❖ Cover and leave to cool for 1 hour so that the mixture is easier to work with.

❖ Feed the mixture through the Sausage Maker Adaptor and cut to convenient lengths. To cook either fry gently, grill or bake.

1 medium onion, finely chopped

15ml (1 tbsp) oil

1 vegetable or chicken stock cube, dissolved in 150ml (¼ pint, ½ cup) hot water

225g (8oz, 4 packed cups) fresh wholemeal breadcrumbs

225g (8oz, 1½ cups) peanuts, ground in the Liquidiser until fine

1 egg

5ml (1 tsp) mixed herbs

freshly milled black pepper

○ *Makes 10 standard sausages*
✗ *Not suitable for freezing*

CHICKEN, LEMON & CHIVE SAUSAGES

450g (1 lb) chicken, skin and bones removed, thigh meat is best

50g (2oz, 1 packed cup) fresh breadcrumbs

5ml (1 tsp) salt

freshly milled black pepper

15ml (1 tbsp) lemon juice

7.5ml (1 heaped tsp) fresh chives, chopped

1 egg

length of sausage casing, standard or small, depending on size of sausage desired, optional

○ *Makes 10 standard or 40 cocktail sausages*

✽ *Suitable for freezing*

❖ Fit the fine screen on to the Mincer attachment and mince the chicken straight into the Kenwood Bowl. Switch off the Chef and remove the Mincer.

❖ Add the remaining ingredients to the minced chicken and mix well using the K Beater at Minimum speed.

❖ Remove any remaining meat from the Mincer, then replace the screen and cutting blade with the Sausage Maker Adaptor and assemble the attachment on the Chef.

❖ Feed the mixture through the adaptor, filling the sausage casing as described on page 66. If preferred you can leave them skinless. These sausages can be fried, grilled or casseroled.

BEEF & BLACK PEPPER SAUSAGES

450g (1lb) shin of beef, bones removed

50g (2oz, 1 packed cup) fresh breadcrumbs

5ml (1 tsp) salt

10ml (2 tsp) freshly milled black pepper

5ml (1 tsp) mixed herbs

1 egg

length of sausage casing, standard or small, depending on size of sausage desired, optional

○ *Makes 14 standard or 40 cocktail sausages*

✽ *Suitable for freezing*

❖ Fit the coarse screen on to the Mincer attachment and mince the beef directly into the Kenwood Bowl. Switch off the Chef and remove the Mincer.

❖ Add the remaining ingredients to the Bowl and mix together using the K Beater at minimum speed.

❖ Remove any remaining meat from the Mincer, then replace the screen and cutting blade with the Sausage Maker Adaptor and assemble the attachment on the Chef.

❖ Feed the mixture through the adaptor, filling the sausage casing as described on page 66.

❖ These sausages are particularly tasty when barbecued, but taste equally as good fried or grilled. Barbecue for approximately 15 minutes for standard size, 5 minutes for cocktail size.

Middle Eastern Kebbe

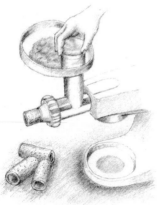

To describe a Kebbe needs more than a few words. It is a traditional Lebanese dish comprising a cylinder-like shell made of meat and bulgur or burghul (cracked wheat). This is then stuffed, traditionally with more meat, spices and other ingredients, and sealed at each end.

To make the outer shell by hand requires a great amount of expertise. It is an arduous task and apparently a female's skill in Kebbe making, requiring long slender fingers, is valued above intellect or beauty.

The Kebbe Maker Adaptor is an accessory which fits on to the Mincer attachment and makes the preparation of Kebbe a whole lot easier, by shaping the outer shell ready for stuffing. The Kebbe mixture is simply fed through the Mincer feed tube and is cut off at intervals as instructed in the recipe.

Hints & Tips

❖ The mixture for making the Kebbe shell often seems quite sticky, but once it has been passed through the Kebbe Maker, becomes quite easy to handle.

❖ Experiment by replacing meat with chicken for a tasty alternative.

Meat Kebbe

100g (4oz, ⅔ cup) bulgur
575ml (1 pint, 2¼ cups) water
325g (12oz) beef or lamb
15ml (1 tbsp) vegetable oil
1 small onion, finely diced
30ml (2 tbsp) pine nuts
2.5ml (½ tsp) ground allspice
salt and freshly milled black pepper
50g (2 oz, ½ cup) plain flour
oil, for deep frying

○ Makes 14 Kebbe balls
✗ Not suitable for freezing

❖ Place the bulgur in a pan and add the water. Bring to the boil and simmer for 15 minutes. Drain, then set to one side until required.

❖ Meanwhile mince the beef or lamb in the Mincer, using the fine screen. Separate 100g (4oz) of the minced meat and put the remainder to one side.

❖ Heat the oil in a pan and sauté the diced onion until golden. Add the pine nuts and sauté for a further 60 seconds to toast. Add the 100g (4oz) minced meat and 1.25ml (¼ tsp) allspice to the pan then fry for about 10 minutes until cooked. Season well with salt and black pepper.

❖ Meanwhile, put the remaining minced meat, drained bulgur, the remaining allspice and a generous amount of seasoning into the Kenwood Bowl. Mix, using the K Beater at speed 1, for 5 minutes. Add the flour and mix at minimum speed to incorporate thoroughly.

- ❖ Remove any remaining meat from the Mincer then replace the screen and cutting blade with the Kebbe Maker Adaptor and assemble the attachment on the Chef.
- ❖ Pass the bulgur mixture through the adaptor, cutting the tubing at 8cm (3") intervals and laying each tube on a tray.
- ❖ To make the Kebbe balls, close one end of the tube, squeezing tightly to seal well, and leaving the other end open. Press 15ml (1 tbsp) of the cooked meat mixture into each shell then squeeze the open end to seal.
- ❖ Heat a pan of oil until moderately hot and deep-fry the Kebbe balls for 3-4 minutes until golden. Serve immediately with a large salad and a spicy yoghurt dressing.

VEGETARIAN KEBBE

This idea breaks with tradition completely, but the result is an excellent vegetarian, crispy-coated ball, suitable for any dinner party.

- ❖ Place the bulgur in a pan and add the water. Bring to the boil and simmer for 15 minutes. Drain and set to one side until needed.
- ❖ Meanwhile, heat the olive oil over a medium heat and sauté the chopped onion and mushrooms for about 25 minutes until they are soft and the liquid has evaporated.
- ❖ Remove from the heat and stir in the pine nuts, grated cheese and parsley. Season to taste with salt and black pepper.
- ❖ Place the drained bulgur in the Kenwood Bowl with the flour and season liberally with salt and black pepper. Use the K Beater at minimum speed for 5 minutes to form a stiff paste.
- ❖ Remove any remaining meat from the Mincer then replace the screen and cutting blade with the Kebbe Maker Adaptor and assemble the attachment on the Chef.
- ❖ Pass the bulgur paste through the adaptor, cutting the tubing at 8cm (3") intervals and laying each tube on a tray.
- ❖ To make the Kebbe balls close one end of the tube, squeezing tightly to seal well, and leaving the other end open. Press 15ml (1 tbsp) of the cooked mushroom mixture into each shell and squeeze the open end to seal.
- ❖ Heat a pan of oil until moderately hot and deep-fry the Kebbe balls for 3-4 minutes until golden. Serve immediately with a large salad and a spicy yoghurt dressing.

225g (8oz, 1 cups) fine bulgur
875ml (1½ pints) water
15ml (1 tbsp) olive oil
1 small onion, finely chopped
175g (6oz) mushrooms, finely chopped
25g (1oz) pine nuts
25g (1oz) vegetarian cheese, grated
15ml (1 tbsp) fresh parsley, chopped
100g (4oz, 1 cup) plain flour
salt and freshly milled black pepper

○ *Makes 14 Kebbe balls*
✗ *Not suitable for freezing*

SLICING & SHREDDING IN SECONDS

"What is more refreshing than salads when your appetite seems to have deserted you, or even after a capacious dinner - the nice, fresh, green, and crisp salad, full of life and health, which seems to invigorate the palate."
Alexis Soyer - A Shilling Cookery for the People

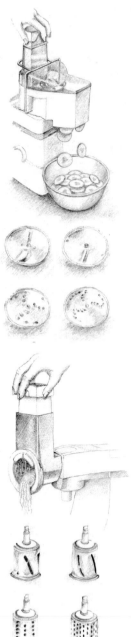

A person whose diet is abundant with fresh produce always looks and feels a picture of health. Their vitality, clear complexion, bright eyes and shining hair is there for all to see.

The Slicer and Shredder has a great affinity with eating plenty of salads and vegetables. It makes light work of preparing carrots, potatoes, onions, cucumber, cabbage and beetroot as well as apples, cheese, chocolate, nuts and can also be used for making ice shavings.

The Chinese population believes that the secret of a well cooked dish relies on the even chopping of its vegetable ingredients. This is so that each individual item will cook at the same rate, ensuring uniform crispness throughout the dish. The same can be applied to cooking worldwide and the Slicer and Shredder performs that task brilliantly.

Another benefit is the time and effort that the Slicer and Shredder can save - a real bonus for preparing a number of dishes for a dinner party or shredding cheese for a fondue. Shredded cheese can be kept in an airtight container in the fridge, so always do more than is necessary to save on preparation at the next meal time.

Both the High Speed and the Slow Speed attachments prepare a large range of ingredients. The High Speed attachment uses flat discs and, as the name implies, slices and shreds the food rapidly. The Slow Speed version uses drums and, being the more traditional one, is simpler in design. There are 2 sizes of slicing and 2 sizes of shredding for each version. All the recipes in this section have been developed for use with either one or both of the attachments as specified in each method.

HINTS & TIPS

❖ Fill the feeder tube before switching on the Chef, as this will achieve the best results.
❖ Make sure items fit the tube tightly for even slices or shreds.
❖ The nut securing the disc on the High Speed attachment can be tightened and untightened using the cleverly designed indentation on top of the pusher.
❖ Use the High Speed attachment at speed 1 and the Slow Speed attachment between speeds 3 and 4.

COOL CRUNCHY COLESLAW

❖ Fit the coarse shredding plate to the High Speed Slicer & Shredder attachment and shred the cabbage, onion and carrot into a bowl.

❖ Sprinkle the salt and 30ml (2 tbsp) of the sugar over the top, then mix well with a large spoon.

❖ Place the white wine vinegar, mustard powder, and oil in a pan. Stir in the remaining sugar and heat until simmering. Pour the liquid over the coleslaw mixture and mix thoroughly to coat. Cover and refrigerate for 1 hour.

❖ Drain the coleslaw in a colander, pressing down to remove as much liquid as possible. This will ensure that it keeps for longer.

❖ Stir in the mayonnaise and season with salt and black pepper to taste.

225g (8oz) white cabbage
1 small Spanish onion, peeled
1 medium carrot, peeled
5ml (1 tsp) salt
75ml (5 tbsp) sugar
60ml (4 tbsp, ¼ cup) white wine vinegar
1.25ml (¼ tsp) mustard powder
30ml (2 tbsp) vegetable oil
150ml (¼ pint, ⅔ cup) mayonnaise
salt and freshly milled black pepper

✪ *Serves 4*
✓ *High Speed Slicer & Shredder*
✗ *Slow Speed Slicer & Shredder*
✗ *Not suitable for freezing*

SWISS CHEESE FONDUE

The ideal way to entertain. For this you need a fondue set complete with long-handled fondue forks. The idea is to skewer a piece of bread or vegetable, dip it into the fondue sauce and twist to coat it well. But beware, tradition says that anyone who drops their bread or vegetable in the sauce has to pay a forfeit! The best part comes at the end when the thick crust which is left on the bottom of the pan is divided between all the guests.

❖ Slice the garlic in half and rub it around the inside of a heavy fondue pan.

❖ Fit the fine shredding plate or drum to the Slicer & Shredder attachment and shred the two cheeses directly into the fondue pan.

❖ Add the wine and nutmeg and place the pan over a low heat.

❖ Stir the fondue until the cheese has melted into the wine. Mix the Kirsh with the cornflour and add this mixture to the pan, stirring continuously until it becomes thick and smooth.

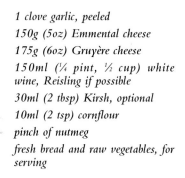

❖ Now the fondue is ready to serve. Place the pan over a burner on the table and surround it with dishes of ready-washed, chopped raw vegetables, and chunks of fresh bread.

1 clove garlic, peeled
150g (5oz) Emmental cheese
175g (6oz) Gruyère cheese
150ml (¼ pint, ½ cup) white wine, Reisling if possible
30ml (2 tbsp) Kirsh, optional
10ml (2 tsp) cornflour
pinch of nutmeg
fresh bread and raw vegetables, for serving

✪ *Serves 4*
✓ *High Speed Slicer & Shredder*
✓ *Slow Speed Slicer & Shredder*
✗ *Not suitable for freezing*

Leek & Potato Pie

This recipe, given to me by a friend, is very simple and utterly delicious - perfect for a family supper served with fish or sausages.

2 large leeks

775g (1¾ lb) potatoes, peeled or scrubbed

25g (1oz, ¼ cup) plain flour

5ml (1 tsp) salt

2.5ml (½ tsp) black pepper, freshly milled

50g (2oz, ¼ cup) butter, cut into small pieces

525ml (18fl oz, 2¼ cups) milk

☐ Oven Temperature 180°C (350°F, gas mark 4)

✿ Serves 4-6

✓ High Speed Slicer & Shredder
✓ Slow Speed Slicer & Shredder
✗ Not suitable for freezing

❖ Preheat the oven. Cut the tops and tails from the leeks, slice in half lengthways and run under cold water. Gently squeeze off the excess water and slice thinly by hand.

❖ Fit the thin slicing plate or drum to the Slicer & Shredder attachment and slice the potatoes into a bowl. You may have to cut some potatoes in half to fit into the feed tube.

❖ Mix together the flour, salt and black pepper. Place one third of the potato slices in a layer in a deep ovenproof baking dish, roughly 23cm x 28cm (9" x 11"). Sprinkle half the leeks, half the seasoned flour and roughly one third of the butter over the surface of the potatoes.

❖ Spread a layer of half the remaining potatoes on top and sprinkle with the rest of the leeks and the seasoned flour. Dot with half the remaining butter. Top with the remaining potato, making sure there is a nice even layer with no leeks showing through, and then dot with the rest of the butter.

❖ Heat the milk until just simmering and pour it over the potatoes.

❖ Cover with a lid or layer of foil and bake for 45 minutes. Remove the foil and bake for a further 15 minutes, to brown the top. Serve hot straight away or allow to cool and re-warm when required.

Potted Gruyère

If you are having a 'proper' dinner party serve little pots of Gruyère with savoury biscuits and port after or instead of dessert - they seem to taste particularly good during the winter months.

225g (8oz) Gruyère cheese

100g (4oz, ½ cup) butter, at room temperature

30ml (2 tbsp) Kirsch

1.25ml (¼ tsp) nutmeg

✿ Serves 8

✓ High Speed Slicer & Shredder
✓ Slow Speed Slicer & Shredder
✗ Not suitable for freezing

❖ Fit the fine shredding plate or drum to the Slicer & Shredder attachment and shred the Gruyère cheese directly into the Kenwood Bowl.

❖ Beat the cheese with the butter, Kirsch and nutmeg for 2 minutes using the K Beater at speed 1.

❖ Press the mixture into individual serving dishes, then cover and leave in a cool place for a few hours to allow the flavours to develop.

CARROT & LEMON SOUP

This soup is really delicious, low in fat and quick to make. With the help of either one of the Slicer and Shredder attachments it can be made in less than 25 minutes, from start to finish.

❖ Preheat the oven. Cut the tops and tails from the leeks, slice in half lengthways and run under cold water. Gently squeeze off the excess water and slice thinly by hand.

❖ Fit either the fine or coarse shredding plate or drum to the Slicer & Shredder attachment and shred the carrots into a bowl.

❖ Heat the oil in a heavy-based pan, add the grated carrot, sliced leek and garlic and allow to sweat for 5 minutes over a gentle heat, while keeping the pan covered. Stir frequently to prevent the vegetables from burning.

❖ Add the lemon zest and stock and simmer for 10 minutes. Remove from the heat and add the lemon juice and fresh parsley. Season to taste with salt and black pepper, then serve immediately.

325g (12oz) carrots, peeled or scraped

30ml (2 tbsp) olive oil

1 small leek

1 small clove garlic, crushed

zest of 1 lemon, grated

725ml (1¼ pints, 2¾ cups) chicken stock

30ml (2 tbsp) lemon juice

30ml (2 tbsp) fresh parsley, chopped

salt and freshly milled black pepper

✪ *Serves 4-6*

✓ *High Speed Slicer & Shredder*

✓ *Slow Speed Slicer & Shredder*

✗ *Not suitable for freezing*

LAYERED SALAD

❖ Fit the thin slicing plate or drum to the Slicer & Shredder attachment. Slice the white and red cabbage, then the cucumber and apple, placing each in layers in a salad bowl.

❖ Change to the fine shredding plate or drum and shred the carrots, cheese and walnuts, layering each in the bowl. Serve with a salad dressing of your choice, or none at all.

¼ white cabbage, stalk removed

¼ red cabbage, stalk

½ cucumber

2 apples, cores removed

2 carrots, peeled or scrubbed

100g (4oz) cheese

50g (2oz, ⅓ cup) walnuts, optional

✪ *Serves 6-8*

✓ *High Speed Slicer & Shredder*

✓ *Slow Speed Slicer & Shredder*

✗ *Not suitable for freezing*

APPLE STRUDEL

675g (1½ lb) cooking apples, peeled and cores removed

225g (8oz, 1½ cups) brown sugar

10ml (2 tsp) mixed spice

100g (4oz, ½ cup) sultanas

45ml (3 tbsp) cornflour

15 sheets filo pastry, measuring 18cm x 32cm (7" x 12½")

25g (1oz, ⅛ cup) butter, melted

☐ Oven Temperature 180°C (350°F, gas mark 4)

✿ Serves 6-8

✓ High Speed Slicer & Shredder
✗ Slow Speed Slicer & Shredder
✗ Not suitable for freezing

❖ Preheat the oven. Fit the coarse shredding plate to the High Speed Slicer & Shredder attachment and shred the apples into a bowl. Add the sugar, spice, sultanas and cornflour and mix together.

❖ Clear a reasonable amount of space on your work surface and lay out 1 sheet of filo pastry leaving enough space to join 4 further sheets onto the 32cm (12½") width. Brush the long edge with a little of the melted butter and join on another sheet to this edge, overlapping by about 2.5cm (1").

❖ Continue with 3 more sheets so that you achieve an overall size of about 80cm x 32cm (32" x 13"). Brush the entire surface with some more of the melted butter and place another layer of 5 filo sheets on top, overlapping the edges as before.

❖ Repeat this process again so that the pastry now has three layers, but still with an 80cm x 32cm (32" x 13") surface area.

❖ Spread the apple mixture over the top of the pastry, leaving a 2.5cm (1") gap all around the edge. Fold all 4 outer edges in so that the filling is not able to leak out.

❖ Carefully roll up the strudel into a log shape about 28cm (11") in width and place on a rimmed baking sheet to retain the juices during cooking. These juices are delicious spooned over the top of the strudel just before serving.

❖ Brush the surface of the roll with the remaining melted butter and bake for 50 minutes. Serve hot with fresh cream or ice cream.

ICE CREAM SPRINKLE

Shredding chocolate produces a beautiful bowl full of shavings which are excellent for decorating cakes. Add nuts and multi-coloured, candy-covered chocolates to transform ice cream into a really colourful, fun dessert.

50g (2oz) plain chocolate

50g (2oz) white chocolate

25g (1oz) almonds or hazelnuts, blanched

50g (2oz, ¼ cup) multi-coloured, candy-covered chocolates

✓ High Speed Slicer & Shredder
✓ Slow Speed Slicer & Shredder
✗ Not suitable for freezing

❖ Fit the fine shredding plate or drum to the Slicer & Shredder attachment. Simply shred all the ingredients into a bowl, then mix together. Use them straight away or keep for up to several weeks in an airtight jar.

Clockwise, from
top right:

Apple Strudel

Layered Salad

Cool Crunchy Coleslaw

Potted Gruyère

Juice - the Healthy Option

We all know that to improve our health we must eat more fruit and vegetables, containing the vitamins and minerals essential for nourishing our bodies. Juicing is a fun way for us to increase our daily intake of these foods, while also enjoying a great variety of raw food that we may otherwise not consume.

Drinking juice drinks at regular periods throughout the day can also help to regulate your body's sugar levels and stave off those pangs of hunger when you are trying to lose weight. Start the day with a fruit juice and some high fibre cereal and you won't feel nearly so hungry for sweets or snacks at coffee time.

There are two attachments for making juice with the Kenwood Chef. The Juice Centrifuge can be used for juicing all types of fruit and vegetable. It operates at high speed to separate the juice from the pulp and can even be used to finely grate coconut for cooking and to extract the starch from potatoes.

Citrus fruits can also be juiced using the Centrifuge, but you must make sure that beforehand you remove both the peel and the white pith which otherwise give the juice a very bitter taste. The specially designed Citrus Juicer makes extracting citrus juice far easier as you only need halve the fruit and hold it over the rotating reamer.

Not all the benefits from juice are visible on the outside – many scientists are now researching the possibilities that certain vitamins and minerals, naturally present in fruit and vegetables, can help protect our bodies against degenerative diseases such as cancer. The table opposite is a guide to vitamins and minerals contained in the most common fruits and vegetables to help you select what your body needs most.

Hints & Tips

❖ The Juice Centrifuge can be dismantled for washing - make sure you don't immerse the base in water. Remove any staining marks with olive oil.

❖ The top of the pusher has an in-built tool for unscrewing the grater inside.

❖ Use the Citrus Juicer for extracting the pulp from large ripe tomatoes (firstly slicing off the base). The tomato shells can then be filled with savoury mousse and served as an appetizing starter.

❖ Use the Juice Centrifuge at speed 1 and the Citrus Juicer at speed 4.

A Guide to Vitamins & Minerals

FOOD	VITAMINS						MINERALS			
	A	B1	B2	B6	C	E	Calcium	Iron	Magnesium	Potassium
Apple									●	
Apricot	●								●	
Asparagus	●									
Blackberries								●		
Blackcurrants					●					
Broccoli	●		●		●					
Cabbage	●		●		●		●	●		●
Carrot	●	●	●	●	●	●	●	●		●
Cauliflower							●			
Celery		●	●	●		●	●			●
Cherry								●	●	
Fennel					●					●
Grapefruit					●					
Grapes								●	●	●
Guava					●					
Kiwi Fruit					●	●				
Lemon					●		●			
Lettuce	●		●			●	●			
Lime					●		●		●	
Melon	●		●		●				●	
Orange					●		●		●	
Parsley	●				●					●
Peach	●				●		●		●	
Pear								●	●	
Pepper – Green					●		●			●
Pepper – Red	●	●	●	●						
Pineapple					●					●
Plum								●	●	
Potato				●						
Radish							●			
Rhubarb	●						●			
Spinach	●		●			●		●	●	
Spring Greens		●					●	●	●	●
Strawberries	●				●			●		
Tomato	●	●	●	●	●	●				●
Watercress		●	●		●	●	●	●	●	

DRINKS

TROPICAL SPRITZER

❖ Juice the mango and pineapple in the Juice Centrifuge. Stir in the Malibu and pour over ice to serve.

½ mango, peeled, with stone removed

2 slices pineapple, skin removed

15ml (1 tbsp) Malibu, coconut liqueur

ice, for serving

○ *Makes 1 glass*

✓ *Juice Centrifuge*

✗ *Citrus Juicer*

✗ *Not suitable for freezing*

MORNING BRIGHT EYE

❖ Juice the ingredients in the Juice Centrifuge and drink first thing in the morning to cleanse the system.

2 apples, washed and quartered (no need to peel or core)

2 large carrots, washed

○ *Makes 1 glass*

✓ *Juice Centrifuge*

✗ *Citrus Juicer*

✗ *Not suitable for freezing*

PEAR & PINEAPPLE DROP

❖ Juice the ingredients in the Juice Centrifuge, stir and serve.

1 pear, washed and quartered (no need to peel or core)

1 slice fresh pineapple, skin removed

○ *Makes 1 glass*

✓ *Juice Centrifuge*

✗ *Citrus Juicer*

✗ *Not suitable for freezing*

SUMMER COOLER

❖ Juice the ingredients in the given order using the Juice Centrifuge and serve with ice.

½ cucumber, washed

2 apples, washed and quartered (no need to peel or core)

mint leaves

1 stick celery, washed

○ *Makes 1 glass*

✓ *Juice Centrifuge*

✗ *Citrus Juicer*

✗ *Not suitable for freezing*

CITRUS REFRESHER

❖ Halve the fruits and extract the juice using the Citrus Juicer. Pour the juice into a bowl and add the sugar.

❖ Pour in the boiling water and stir well to mix. Cover and chill for a couple of hours then serve with ice and a slice of lemon.

1 orange

1 lime

1 lemon

1 grapefruit

175g (6oz, ¾ cup) sugar, brown or white

875ml (1½ pints, 3½ cups) boiling water

❂ *Serves 8-10*

✗ *Juice Centrifuge*

✓ *Citrus Juicer*

✗ *Not suitable for freezing*

FIZZY LEMONADE

A friend came up with the suggestion of making a lemonade concentrate which could be diluted with sparkling water to make a fizzy lemonade. The result was delicious. The concentrate lasts for up to one week if kept in a capped bottle in the refrigerator.

❖ Halve the lemons and extract the juice using the Citrus Juicer. Pour the juice into a small pan and add the sugar.

❖ Heat gently, stirring continuously until the sugar has dissolved. Pour into a glass bottle with a lid, and leave to cool.

❖ To serve pour a little of the concentrate into a glass and top with sparkling mineral water, according to taste.

4 lemons

225g (8oz, 1½ cups) brown sugar

sparkling mineral water, chilled

○ *Makes 10-12 servings*

✗ *Juice Centrifuge*

✓ *Citrus Juicer*

✗ *Not suitable for freezing*

Sweet Desserts

Fresh Orange Jelly

5 oranges, for 300ml
(½ pint, 1¼ cups) juice
7.5ml (1½ tsp) gelatine powder
30ml (2 tbsp) sugar

✿ *Serves 4*
✗ *Juice Centrifuge*
✓ *Citrus Juicer*
✗ *Not suitable for freezing*

❖ Halve the oranges and extract the juice with the Citrus Juicer using as many oranges as required to obtain a 300ml (½ pint, 1¼ cups) quantity.

❖ Heat a quarter of the juice in a small pan, adding the gelatine and sugar and stirring constantly. When the liquid has reached simmering point and the gelatine has dissolved, remove the pan from the heat and stir in the remaining orange juice.

❖ Pour into a jelly mould or serving dishes, then cover and leave to cool. Place in the refrigerator to set. Serve Orange Jelly on its own, with fresh cream or with ice cream.

Melon Balls in Juice

1 melon, ripened
30ml (2 tbsp) fructose, optional if
the melon is not sweet enough

✿ *Serves 4*
✓ *Juice Centrifuge*
✗ *Citrus Juicer*
✗ *Not suitable for freezing*

❖ Wash the melon and dry with a paper towel. Halve it and remove the pips. Scoop out as many whole balls as you can and put them into a chilled serving dish.

❖ Cut the remaining melon into pieces, leaving the rind intact as this gives a lovely creamy texture to the juice.

❖ Juice the melon pieces in the Juice Centrifuge and pour over the melon balls. Taste and add the fructose if you prefer a sweeter taste.

❖ Refrigerate for at least two hours before serving.

ORANGE & LEMON CURD

❖ Finely grate the zest from the lemon and orange then place in a medium-sized heatproof bowl.

❖ Halve the lemon and orange then extract the juice using the Citrus Juicer. Add this to the bowl, then stir in the brown sugar, eggs and butter.

❖ Place the bowl over a pan of barely simmering water and stir for 15-20 minutes until the curd is both hot and thickened.

❖ Pour into sterilised clean, warm jars and seal. Leave to cool then store in a refrigerator. Serve with bread, toast or as a filling for sponge cakes.

1 lemon, washed and dried
1 orange, washed and dried
175g (6oz, 1 cup) brown sugar
3 eggs, beaten
100g (4oz, ½ cup) butter, cut into pieces

○ *Makes 2 jars*
✗ *Juice Centrifuge*
✓ *Citrus Juicer*
✗ *Not suitable for freezing*

CREOLE COCONUT PIE

A delicious pie made from the pulp of a fresh coconut - the Juice Centrifuge does it all!

❖ Preheat the oven. Pierce the eyes of the coconut and drain out the coconut milk. Put this to one side then remove the outer shell of the coconut.

❖ Break the coconut into pieces and put through the Juice Centrifuge (brown skin as well), bearing in mind that you are collecting both the pulp and the juice.

❖ Next make the pastry case. Use the K Beater at minimum speed to mix together the flour, butter and 15ml (1 tbsp) of the coconut pulp until it turns to crumbs. Add enough of the reserved coconut milk to the mixture to form a ball.

❖ Press the mixture into a 23cm (9") flan tin.

❖ Combine the coconut pulp with the remaining ingredients, including the thicker coconut milk which was produced when making the pulp, and pour the mixture into the pastry shell.

❖ Bake for 45 minutes until the filling is set. Serve either warm or cold, both ways are delicious.

1 fresh coconut
100g (4oz, 1 cup) plain flour
50g (2oz, ¼ cup) butter
3 eggs
30ml (2 tbsp) natural yoghurt
30ml (2 tbsp) milk
5ml (1 tsp) vanilla essence
175g (6oz, ¾ cup) caster sugar

○ *Makes 1 x 23cm (9") tart*
☐ *Oven Temperature 180°C (350°F, gas mark 4)*
✓ *Juice Centrifuge*
✗ *Citrus Juicer*
✳ *Suitable for freezing*

POTATO DISHES

LIGHT POTATO ROSTI

Unlike traditional potato rosti, this recipe uses the ability of the Juice Centrifuge to extract the heavy starch from the potato, making a much lighter meal.

450g (1lb) potatoes, peeled
15ml (1 tbsp) olive oil
5ml (1 tsp) lemon juice
2.5ml (½ tsp) salt
freshly milled black pepper
oil, for shallow-frying

✪ Serves 4
✓ Juice Centrifuge
✗ Citrus Juicer
✗ Not suitable for freezing

❖ Put the potatoes through the Juice Centrifuge and, remembering that you are collecting the pulp, place the Kenwood Bowl under the larger pulp outlet. Collect the juice in a jug, but discard it as it is amazingly heavy in starch.

❖ Mix the pulp with the olive oil and lemon juice, then add the salt and season with black pepper.

❖ Put a little oil into a frying pan and place over a medium heat. Shallow-fry the rosti in 4 patty shapes for 5 minutes on each side.

❖ Serve hot with fish, meat or simply on their own.

SCOTTISH POTATO DROP SCONES

These are quick to make and are really delicious. Like the Potato Rosti they rely on the Juice Centrifuge's ability to make potato pulp which has had all the heavy starch taken out - makes an excellent ingredient.

325g (12oz) potatoes
10ml (2 tsp) sugar
100g (4oz, 1 cup) self raising flour
1 egg
salt and freshly milled black pepper
oil, for shallow frying

◯ Makes 6
✓ Juice Centrifuge
✗ Citrus Juicer
✗ Not suitable for freezing

❖ Put the potatoes through the Juice Centrifuge and, remembering that you are collecting the pulp, place the Kenwood Bowl under the larger pulp outlet. Collect the juice in a jug, but discard it as it is heavy in starch.

❖ Add the sugar, flour and egg to the pulp, season with salt and pepper and mix at a low speed with the K Beater.

❖ Pour a little oil into a frying pan and place over a medium heat. Divide the potato mixture into 6 scones.

❖ Put the scones into the pan, flattening them slightly, and fry for 5 minutes on each side. Serve hot with butter and maple syrup or honey.

MULTIPLE USES FOR THE MULTI MILL

The Multi Mill represents 3 products in 1. First and foremost it is a mini 'mill', for milling hard items such as curry spices, peppercorns and coffee beans.

Secondly it acts as a mini 'chopper', the sharp blades being able to chop small items such as onion, garlic or parsley which is so awkward to do by hand.

Its third function is as a mini 'blender'. Its miniature size makes it ideal for puréeing small quantities of food which otherwise become lost at the base of a conventional blender. Curry paste, pesto, nut butters, fruit purées, salad dressings are just a few examples of the preparations it can make.

The most ingenious thing about this attachment is that the milling jar has an airtight lid so that when the preparation is ready you can cap it and store it. Four jars are supplied with the Multi Mill when it is bought individually. They make handy containers for all sorts of things, so you may want to buy extra. As they are made of glass, aromas can't linger, unlike with many plastic storage containers, which is important when using aromatic spices.

When it comes to feeding our babies we may often open a jar of commercially-prepared food, not really knowing the source of its ingredients, or how it has been made. The Multi Mill offers an easy solution - it is excellent for puréeing just the right quantity of food for youngsters, whether it is specially prepared or taken from your own meal. You can even prepare several meals at one time and freeze them - great for busy working parents.

HINTS & TIPS

❖ It is always a good idea to label and date food for storage.

❖ When making baby food, current advice tells us not to add salt to the preparation as enough salt is present naturally in the foods we consume. If in doubt always consult your doctor first.

❖ Use the Multi Mill at maximum speed.

NINETEENTH CENTURY RECIPE FOR SALAD DRESSING

"Two large potatoes, passed through the kitchen sieve,
Unwonted softness to the salad give;
Of mordent mustard, add a single spoon,
Distrust the condiment which bites too soon;
But deem it not, thou man of herbs, a fault,
To add a double quantity of salt;
Three times the spoon with oil of Lucca crown,
And once with vinegar, procured from the town;
True flavour needs it, and your poet begs
The pounded yellow of two well-boiled eggs;
Let onion atoms lurk within the bowl,
And scarce suspected animate the whole;
And lastly, in the flavoured compound toss
A magic teaspoon of anchovy sauce:
Then, though green turtle fail, though venison's tough,
And ham and turkey are not boiled enough,
Serenely full, the epicure may say –
Fate cannot harm me – I have dined today."
REVEREND SYDNEY SMITH

At first sight you might wonder why this salad dressing has not been made in the Colander & Sieve. This method does indeed give great results, but the Multi Mill produces a dressing more like a potato mayonnaise which is lovely with boiled eggs, salads and fish. Here is the recipe roughly translated and halved in quantity.

❖ Place all the ingredients, except the onion, in the Multi Mill and blend until very smooth.

❖ Spoon the preparation into a bowl and stir in the chopped onion. This salad dressing can be eaten immediately or can be kept in the refrigerator for up to 24 hours.

1 medium potato, peeled and boiled

5ml (1 tsp) mustard

5ml (1 tsp) salt

60ml (4 tbsp) olive oil

22.5ml (1½ tbsp) white wine vinegar

1 hard-boiled egg, yolk only

5ml (1 tsp) anchovy essence

1 small onion, finely chopped

✪ *Serves 4*

✗ *Not suitable for freezing*

West Indian Chicken with Cashew Nut Butter

45ml (3 tbsp) vegetable oil
2 medium onions, cubed
3 large cloves garlic, crushed
10ml (2 tsp) fresh ginger, grated
45ml (3 tbsp) curry powder
5ml (1 tsp) chilli powder
3 tomatoes
8 chicken thighs, weighing
1.4-1.8kg (3-4 lb)
300ml (½ pint, 1¼ cups) chicken stock
100g (4oz, 1 cup) cashew nuts
30ml (2 tbsp) yoghurt
10ml (2 tsp) ground coriander
salt and freshly milled black pepper

✪ *Serves 4-6*
✳ *Suitable for freezing*

❖ Heat the oil in a large pan and sauté the onions, garlic and ginger over a medium heat for 20-30 minutes until they turn a deep golden colour. Add the curry and chilli powder and fry for 1 minute.

❖ Meanwhile, quarter the tomatoes and blend them in the Multi Mill, in batches if necessary, until smooth. Add to the pan with the chicken thighs and stir to coat the chicken well.

❖ Pour in the stock, cover the pan and simmer gently for 45 minutes, or until the chicken is cooked through. Stir occasionally to prevent the chicken from sticking to the base of the pan.

❖ Using the Multi Mill, chop the cashew nuts until they are very fine, almost to the point of becoming a nut butter.

❖ Stir the freshly chopped nuts, yoghurt and coriander into the chicken and heat through. Check and season if necessary with salt and black pepper, then serve.

Chicken Tikka Kebabs

450g (1 lb) chicken breast, skin and bones removed
10ml (2 tsp) ground coriander
10ml (2 tsp) ground cumin
½ small onion, peeled and roughly chopped
1 clove garlic, peeled
10g (½ oz) fresh ginger, peeled and roughly chopped
30ml (2 tbsp) lemon juice
10ml (2 tsp) paprika
2.5ml (½ tsp) chilli powder, optional
5ml (1 tsp) salt
15ml (1 tbsp) fresh coriander
45ml (3 tbsp) yoghurt

◯ *Makes 12 skewers, suitable for a buffet or 4 skewers as a main course*
✳ *Suitable for freezing*

❖ Cut the chicken into evenly-sized pieces, 2cm x 2cm (1" x 1") and put them into a bowl which will not be tainted by spices.

❖ Place the remaining ingredients, except the yoghurt, in the Multi Mill and blend until smooth.

❖ Pour the sauce over the chicken, add the yoghurt and stir well to make sure the chicken is well-coated in the marinade.

❖ Cover and leave for 12-24 hours in a cool place.

❖ Thread pieces of chicken on to either wooden or metal skewers. Use 4 pieces on each of the 12 skewers for a buffet, or divide the chicken pieces evenly between 4 skewers for a main course.

❖ If you are using wooden skewers, cover the exposed wood with some tin foil to stop them burning.

❖ Grill under a very hot grill for 3 minutes on one side and 2 minutes on the other. They can also be barbecued. Serve with salad and rice.

STUFFED MUSSELS

So often mussels are stuffed with huge amounts of butter and garlic which, although mouth-watering, is a little predictable. This dish makes an excellent first course - and no butter in sight!

❖ Begin by cleaning the mussel shells and removing the beards. Discard any mussels which have damaged shells or are not firmly shut.

❖ Put the water in a large pan and bring to the boil. Place the mussels in batches in the water and cook until they open their shells. Each batch should contain just enough mussels to cover the surface of the water, allowing room for them to open easily. It is important to remove the cooked mussels from the water as soon as they open because if left, they become rubbery. Put each batch of mussels to one side to drain and cool while you cook the next batch.

❖ When all the mussels are cooked, make the stuffing by firstly placing the pine nuts in the Multi Mill and chopping until they become crumbs. Empty them out into a bowl.

❖ Now put the tomatoes, basil, olive oil, lemon juice, sugar and garlic into the Multi Mill in the above order and blend until smooth.

❖ Pour the preparation onto the ground pine nuts, season with salt and black pepper and stir it all together.

❖ You are now ready to stuff the mussels. Pull the shells apart, discarding one half of the shell, so that you are left with a mussel in a boat, then top with 5ml (1 tsp) of the mixture. Place on a wire grill or rack to prevent the mussels from slipping around. Continue until all the mussels have been stuffed.

❖ The stuffed mussels can now be refrigerated for a few hours, covered with plastic film or cooked straight away. To cook, grill under the highest setting for 2-3 minutes until bubbling. Serve with crusty bread.

900g (2 lb) live mussels
1.25 litres (2 pints) water, for cooking
50g (2oz, ⅓ cup) pine nuts
2 tomatoes, quartered, skins removed
10g (½oz) fresh basil
30ml (2 tbsp) olive oil
5ml (1 tsp) lemon juice
pinch of sugar
1 clove garlic
salt and freshly milled black pepper

✪ Serves 4, as a first course
✗ Not suitable for freezing

PESTO SAUCE

25g (1oz, ⅓ cup) Parmesan
cheese, grated
10g (½oz) fresh basil
40g (1½oz, ⅓ cup) cashew nuts
45ml (3 tbsp) olive oil
salt and freshly milled black
pepper

✪ Serves 2
✗ Not suitable for freezing

❖ Place all the ingredients in the Multi Mill and blend until smooth. Season to taste with salt and black pepper and serve with pasta, soup, fish or chicken. Pesto will keep for up to 1 week if refrigerated in the Multi Mill jar with its lid on.

BANANA & YOGHURT BABY PUDDING

The Multi Mill is excellent for baby foods - this pudding is so silky smooth it is ideal for first stage food.

½ banana, peeled
30ml (2 tbsp) yoghurt
5ml (1 tsp) honey, optional

○ Makes 1 jar, enough for 1
meal
✳ Suitable for freezing

❖ Cut the banana into three and blend in the Multi Mill until smooth. Add the yoghurt and honey and blend again. Serve immediately.

AVOCADO & CUCUMBER FACE PACK

A slightly unusual use for the Multi Mill, you might think, but I certainly had great fun testing this recipe. My skin definitely felt soft and refreshed after using it, on both my face and hands. It's best to use the mixture straight away so invite a friend to join in.

½ avocado
1cm (½") piece cucumber, washed
15ml (1 tbsp) yoghurt
4 thin slices cucumber, for placing
over your eyes, optional

○ Makes enough for 2 treatments
of face and hands
✗ Not suitable for freezing

❖ Make sure your Multi Mill is very clean. Peel the avocado, remove the stone and quarter.
❖ Place the avocado with the cucumber and yoghurt in the Multi Mill then blend until smooth. Spread over your face, avoiding the delicate eye area which you can cover with the cucumber slices.
❖ Relax for 5 minutes then rinse off with tepid water.

ALL ABOUT PASTA

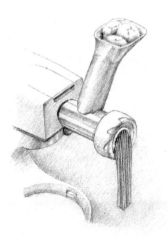

Some say Marco Polo, the 15th century explorer, brought the first pasta to the west from China. Others say it is not possible to record one single historical origin. Pasta is, however, one of the most ancient of foods and even appears in a cookery book written in the first century AD, attributed to Apicus, a gastronome of that time.

Today, it is the Italians who are responsible for the current trend in pasta and it is they who must be credited for having the widest and shapeliest range of pasta available. Pasta is not only healthy and nutritious but is also the great new stamina food, frequently eaten by athletes and marathon runners before a race.

All pasta connoisseurs whether they be Italian, Chinese or any other nationality, will agree that the best pasta, in terms of flavour and texture, is fresh pasta made at home using eggs. This pasta is known as *al ouvo* in Italian, or *mien* in Chinese. This is the type of pasta that you can make with the Pasta Extruder.

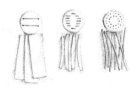

Using the Pasta Extruder is quick, simple and fun and, as it extrudes rather than rolls, offers a greater variety of shapes. There are 6 screens for making spaghetti, small and large macaroni, rigatoni, tagliatelle, lasagne and large macaroni.

Traditionally, Italian pasta is made with the hard Durham wheat flour (semolina) but all of these recipes can be made using any standard variety of flour. You can also experiment with wholemeal or any other types of flour made using the Grain Mill. Making colourful pasta is just as easy – try the red, or green pasta, or even the jet black pasta (*Pasta al Nero di Seppia*) using squid ink.

HINTS & TIPS

❖ Use the tool supplied to push the pasta mixture down the attachment tube. The other end acts as a spanner for untightening the ring nut when you need to remove or change the screens.

❖ The easiest way to clean the attachment is to firstly take it apart. Leave all the pieces to dry overnight or even place in the freezer for an hour. Scrape off the dried pasta from the tube and the scroll and push out the pieces from the screens using the wire tool supplied.

❖ Use the Pasta Maker between speeds 1-3.

BASIC PASTA RECIPES

To make 1 quantity (enough for 4-6 servings) of fresh pasta using the Pasta Extruder

Plain Pasta

500g (1lb 2oz, 3¾ cups) plain flour
2.5ml (½ tsp) salt
4 eggs
2.5ml (½ tsp) oil

Herb Pasta

500g (1lb 2oz, 3¾ cups) plain flour
2.5ml (½ tsp) salt
4 eggs
2.5ml (½ tsp) oil
60ml (4 tbsp) mixed fresh herbs,
finely chopped

Wholemeal Pasta

500g (1lb 2oz, 3¾ cups) wholemeal flour
2.5ml (½ tsp) salt
4 eggs
2.5ml (½ tsp) oil
15ml (1 tbsp) extra water, to be added after
measuring up to the beaker line

Pasta Rossa

500g (1lb 2oz, 3¾ cups) plain flour
2.5ml (½ tsp) salt
3 eggs
2.5ml (½ tsp) oil
75g (3oz, ⅔ cup) tomato purée

Pasta al Nero di Seppia

500g (1lb 2oz, 3¾ cups) plain flour
2.5ml (½ tsp) salt
3 eggs
3 sachets black squid ink concentrate, available from
good fishmongers
2.5ml (½ tsp) oil

Pasta Verde

500g (1lb 2oz, 3¾ cups) plain flour
2.5ml (½ tsp) salt
2 eggs
2.5ml (½ tsp) oil
150g (6oz, 1⅓ cups) puréed spinach

PREPARATION

❖ Place the flour and salt in the Kenwood Bowl. If you are making Herb Pasta add the herbs as well.

❖ Put the eggs and oil into the measuring Beaker supplied with the attachment. Add water if necessary to reach the appropriate line on the Beaker. If you are making coloured pasta, add the extra colouring ingredient at this stage.

❖ Beat the egg mixture together using a fork and add to the flour in the Kenwood Bowl.

❖ Use the K Beater at minimum speed to thoroughly incorporate the mixture. The Pasta mixture should be fairly dry and resemble breadcrumbs.

❖ Pass the mixture through the Pasta Extruder using the desired screen (full details for usage can be found in the Pasta Extruder instruction leaflet).

COOKING

Add 15ml (1 tbsp) salt to a large pan of boiling water (water for cooking pasta should taste salty like the sea). Gradually add the pasta and cook at a slow 'rolling' boil, stirring occasionally until it is 'al dente' or still slightly firm to bite. This will be approximately 8-12 minutes, according to the shape of the pasta. Drain thoroughly before serving. Cooled cooked pasta can be revitalised by soaking in boiling water for 1 to 2 minutes.

STORAGE

Rigatoni and Macaroni must be cooked within 4 hours. Spaghetti, Tagliatelle and Lasagne may be cooked immediately, left to dry, or placed in a plastic bag for freezing.

NB.

These instructions and recipes may differ slightly from those given in the standard instruction leaflet. Both methods are correct and can be used according to your own preference.

VEGETARIAN LENTIL LASAGNE

Lasagne is an excellent dinner party dish. This recipe breaks with tradition, however, by using Puy lentils - a really healthy alternative.

LENTIL FILLING:

30ml (2 tbsp) olive oil

2 cloves garlic, crushed

1 carrot, peeled and diced

2 sticks celery, diced

1 small onion, peeled and finely chopped

4 tomatoes, halved with skins removed

875ml (1½ pints, 3½ cups) vegetable stock

2 sprigs of fresh thyme

225g (8oz, 1⅓ cups) Puy lentils

salt and freshly milled black pepper

CHEESE SAUCE:

50g (2oz, ¼ cup) butter

25g (1oz, ¼ cup) plain flour

425ml (¾ pint, 1¾ cups) milk

100g (4oz, 1⅓ cups) medium hard vegetarian cheese, or Gruyère for non-strict vegetarians, grated

5ml (1 tsp) nutmeg, freshly grated

PASTA:

½ quantity of fresh Lasagne (see p.95 for preparation)

☐ *Oven Temperature 180°C (400°F, gas mark 4)*

✿ *Serves 6*

✳ *Suitable for freezing*

❖ Heat the oil in a large pan, then sauté the garlic, carrot, celery and onion for 15 minutes until they are a deep golden colour.

❖ Add the tomatoes and sauté for a further 10 minutes until the tomatoes have turned to a pulp and the liquid has evaporated. Add the stock, thyme and lentils, then cover and simmer, for 45 minutes or until the lentils are cooked. Season well with salt and black pepper.

❖ Meanwhile, make the sauce by firstly heating the butter until it starts to bubble. Add the flour, stirring well, then allow the mixture to fry for 2 minutes.

❖ Remove the pan from the heat and allow to cool a little before adding the milk, stirring constantly to achieve a smooth texture. Return to the heat and bring to the boil again, stirring continuously until the sauce thickens.

❖ Simmer for 2 minutes then remove from the heat once again. Stir in half the grated cheese, and season well with the nutmeg, salt and black pepper.

❖ If you are dining straight away, preheat the oven then butter an ovenproof dish. Spread a layer of lentil mixture over the base.

❖ Place a single layer of uncooked Lasagne over the top, then cover with another layer of lentil mixture. Pour on roughly half the cheese sauce and spread over the surface.

❖ Add another layer of Lasagne, followed by the lentil mixture and finally pour on the remaining cheese sauce. Sprinkle the top with the remaining cheese.

❖ If you intend to freeze the dish, do so now before it is baked, but remember to defrost it thoroughly before use. Bake for 45 minutes until the cheese topping starts to bubble. Serve with a green salad and garlic bread.

ORIENTAL CHICKEN & CASHEW NUT SALAD

❖ Mix together the sesame oil, ground coriander and chilli powder to make a marinade. Slice the chicken breast very thinly and coat with the marinade, then cover and leave for 30 minutes.

❖ Heat the vegetable oil in a frying pan until it is very hot. Add the marinated chicken and stir-fry for 3 minutes until golden. Season lightly with salt and black pepper, then transfer from the frying pan on to kitchen paper to blot off excess oil. Place in a bowl.

❖ Put the mangetout and fresh coriander into the pan and stir-fry for 1 minute until the mangetout is a vibrant green. Add to the chicken.

❖ Lastly, place the cashew nuts in the pan and stir-fry for 1 minute until toasted, then add to the chicken.

❖ Cook the Spaghetti until 'al dente', using the method given on page 95.

❖ Meanwhile, make the dressing by heating the oils together in a small pan. Add the garlic and ginger, then sauté until golden before stirring in the soy sauce and lemon juice. Bring to simmering point and remove from the heat.

❖ Drain the pasta then stir in the dressing and the chicken mixture. Sprinkle with more fresh coriander and serve either hot or cold.

SALAD:

5ml (1 tsp) sesame oil

5ml (1 tsp) ground coriander

2.5ml (½ tsp) chilli powder

325g (12oz) chicken breast, skin and bones removed

30ml (2 tbsp) vegetable oil

salt and freshly milled black pepper

100g (4oz) mangetout

30ml (2 tbsp) fresh coriander, chopped

25g (1oz, ¼ cup) cashew nuts

½ quantity of fresh Spaghetti (see p.95 for preparation)

DRESSING:

45ml (3 tbsp) vegetable oil

10ml (2 tsp) sesame oil

1 clove garlic, crushed

5ml (1 tsp) fresh ginger, grated

15ml (1 tbsp) dark soy sauce

15ml (1 tbsp) lemon juice

✪ *Serves 2-4*

✗ *Not suitable for freezing*

THREE TOMATO & FETA RIGATONI

❖ Gently sauté the onion in the oil for 5 minutes until softened. Add the garlic and cook for a further 2 minutes.

❖ Stir in the canned and sun-dried tomatoes and simmer gently for 10 minutes, stirring occasionally until the sauce thickens.

❖ Add the cherry tomato halves, season to taste with salt and black pepper, and simmer for a further 2 minutes.

❖ Meanwhile, cook the Rigatoni until 'al dente' using the method given on page 95. Drain and tip into a large, warmed serving bowl.

❖ Add the prepared tomato Sauce and the Feta cheese and stir gently to coat the pasta. Serve with a large salad.

1 medium onion, chopped

15ml (1 tbsp) olive oil

2 cloves garlic, crushed

1 x 400g (14oz) can chopped tomatoes

60ml (4 tbsp) sun-dried tomatoes, finely chopped

150g (5oz) cherry tomatoes, halved

salt and freshly milled black pepper

¾ quantity of fresh Rigatoni (see p.95 for preparation)

225g (8oz) Feta cheese, cubed

✪ *Serves 4-6*

✗ *Not suitable for freezing*

TAGLIATELLE WITH CHICKEN LIVER, CAPERS & SAGE

30ml (2 tbsp) vegetable oil
1 medium onion, peeled and finely chopped
1 carrot, peeled and diced
1 stick celery, diced
225g (8oz) chicken livers, defrosted if frozen
1 x 400g (14oz) can chopped tomatoes
15ml (1 tbsp) tomato purée
5ml (1 tsp) sugar
2.5ml (½ tsp) white wine vinegar
salt and freshly milled black pepper
15ml (1 tbsp) capers, drained and chopped
2.5ml (½ tsp) dried sage
¼ quantity of fresh Tagliatelle (see p.95 for preparation)

✪ *Serves 4*
✗ *Not suitable for freezing*

❖ Heat the oil over a medium heat and add the onion, carrot and celery. Sauté for 20-25 minutes, stirring occasionally until golden.

❖ Finely chop the chicken livers. The easiest way is to put the livers into a bowl and use a pair of kitchen scissors to cut them into pieces. Add the chopped chicken livers to the pan and sauté for 5 minutes.

❖ Pour in the chopped tomatoes, tomato purée, sugar and white wine vinegar. Season with salt and a generous sprinkling of black pepper and simmer gently, uncovered, for 15 minutes.

❖ Stir in the capers and sage then simmer for a further 5 minutes.

❖ Meanwhile, cook the Tagliatelle until 'al dente', using the method given on page 95.

❖ Drain the Tagliatelle and tip into a large, warmed serving dish. Add the sauce, stir it all together and serve immediately with a large salad.

MACARONI WITH RAISINS & APRICOT

¼ quantity of fresh Macaroni (see p.95 for preparation)
525ml (18fl oz, 2 cups) milk
300ml (10fl oz, 1¼ cups) single cream
zest of 1 lemon, grated
50g (2oz, ⅓ cup) soft brown sugar
100g (4oz, ⅔ cup) raisins
50g (2oz, ½ cup) dried apricots, soaked overnight, drained and chopped
5ml (1 tsp) nutmeg, grated

☐ *Oven Temperature 190ºC (350ºF, gas mark 4)*
✪ *Serves 4*
✗ *Not suitable for freezing*

❖ Place the Macaroni, milk, cream and lemon zest in a large saucepan, and bring to the boil, stirring occasionally.

❖ Simmer the mixture for 30 minutes, or until the Macaroni is very soft.

❖ Preheat the oven. Remove the pan from the heat and stir in the raisins and apricots, mixing them with the Macaroni until the sugar has dissolved.

❖ Spoon the mixture into a lightly greased dish, and sprinkle with the nutmeg.

❖ Bake, uncovered, for 30 minutes, or until the top is golden brown. Serve hot or cold according to taste.

Great Uses for the Colander, Sieve, or Potato Ricer

Sieving food seems to release a flavour and aroma to the dish which is very delicate and exquisite. It may be because the food has been pressed and therefore all the natural oils and juices have been released, or it may be because the texture is perfectly even. Whatever the reason, the results certainly speak for themselves.

The texture and appearance of the food we eat is very important and a perfectly smooth purée certainly has its place when creating a balance of flavours, colours and consistency during a meal. Our enormous love for puréed and sieved dishes probably stems from babyhood when our first introduction to adult food was always silky smooth.

When a dish needs to be even in texture it is very important that it is just that – lumpy mashed potato still haunts me from my school days! The Colander & Sieve has a rotating paddle which makes light work of any sieving or puréeing. It is supplied with two screens, each with a rough and a smooth side to give four possible textures ranging from coarse to very fine. The Colander & Sieve purées fruit or cooked vegetables, makes biscuits into crumbs, removes pips and stones from fruits and is also a wonderful attachment for creating clear soups and sifting flour.

Hints & Tips

❖ The two plates can be used together at the same time to achieve an extra smooth result – this is particularly useful if the food contains tiny pips that need to be removed.

❖ Make sure the paddles reach far enough down so that they push tightly onto the sieving screen, yet they retain a slight flex. The paddle can be adjusted if necessary by altering the tightness of the screw at the top of the shaft.

❖ Use the smooth side of the fine screen to sift flour into the Bowl when making cakes or bread.

❖ Use the Colander & Sieve between speeds 1 to 2.

CELERIAC PURÉE

This is my favourite purée. Serve it with any meat, fish or vegetarian meal. It is especially good with sausages.

❖ Preheat the oven, if you are to be using this method of cooking. Put the cubes of celeriac and potato into a pan and pour boiling water over them. Season with the salt. Cover and simmer for 10-15 minutes until the vegetables are soft.

❖ Drain and allow to cool slightly. Sieve the vegetables, using the rough side of the coarse screen, into the Bowl.

❖ Stir in the crème fraîche and season well with salt and black pepper. Return to the pan to reheat over a low setting, or empty into a baking dish, cover and place in the oven for 15 minutes.

❖ Scoop the potato directly onto plates for serving.

450g (1 lb) celeriac, peeled and cut into 2.5cm (1") cubes

450g (1 lb) potatoes, peeled and cut into 4cm (1½") cubes

boiling water, for cooking

5ml (1 tsp) salt

15ml (1 tbsp) crème fraîche

salt and freshly milled black pepper

☐ *Oven Temperature 190°C (375°F, gas mark 5)*

✪ *Serves 4*

✗ *Not suitable for freezing*

POTATO PURÉE WITH A HINT OF GARLIC & OLIVE OIL

❖ Preheat the oven. Put the potatoes into a pan and cover with the boiling water. Add the salt and simmer gently for 10-15 minutes until just cooked.

❖ Drain and allow to cool a little before sieving, using the rough side of the coarse screen.

❖ In a pan, gently heat the olive oil and garlic for 2 or 3 minutes to infuse the flavours. Add the oil and garlic to the potato together with the crème fraîche and butter then season well with salt and black pepper.

❖ Beat, using the K Beater at minimum speed until the potato is smooth. Spoon the mashed potato into an ovenproof dish and bake for 25 minutes until the top is golden and crispy.

❖ Serve scoops of potato as an accompaniment with any main dish, or even as a lunchtime snack on its own.

675g (1½ lb) potatoes, peeled and chopped

boiling water, for cooking

10ml (2 tsp) salt

30ml (2 tbsp) olive oil

1 clove garlic, crushed

15ml (1 tbsp) crème fraîche

10g (½oz) butter, optional

salt and freshly milled black pepper

☐ *Oven Temperature 200°C (400°F, gas mark 6)*

✪ *Serves 4*

✗ *Not suitable for freezing*

SWEET POTATO PURÉE

This purée has a very slight flavour of chestnuts - it is excellent served with any meats that need a sweet accompaniment.

200g (7oz) sweet potatoes, peeled and cut into 2.5cm (1") cubes

boiling water, for cooking

pinch of sugar

2.5ml (½ tsp) salt

10g (½ oz) butter

freshly milled black pepper

☐ *Oven Temperature 180°C (350°F, gas mark 4)*

✪ *Serves 4*

✗ *Not suitable for freezing*

❖ Preheat the oven, if using this method of cooking. Simmer the sweet potatoes in the water, with the sugar and salt added, for 10-15 minutes until tender.

❖ Drain, allow to cool a little then sieve, using the rough side of the coarse screen. Stir in the butter and season with black pepper to taste.

❖ Return to the pan and reheat over a low setting or empty into a baking dish, cover, and place in the oven for 15 minutes.

WINTER VEGETABLE SOUP

Virtually fat free and very warming - a really delicious and healthy soup.

875ml (1½ pints, 3½ cups) vegetable or chicken stock

1 small onion, peeled and sliced

175g (6oz) swede, peeled and cut into 1cm (½") cubes

175g (6oz) turnip, peeled and cut into 1cm (½") cubes

2 carrots, peeled and sliced

225g (8oz) potatoes, peeled and cut into 1.5cm (¾") cubes

5ml (1 tsp) mixed dried herbs

3 tomatoes, halved

boiling water, for cooking

salt and freshly milled black pepper

✪ *Serves 4*

✗ *Not suitable for freezing*

❖ Simply put all the ingredients into a pan, cover with the boiling water and simmer for 45 minutes until the vegetables are tender.

❖ Leave to cool a little, then sieve using the rough side of the coarse screen.

❖ Reheat gently, then season to taste with salt and black pepper. Serve with plenty of fresh wholemeal bread.

FRESH TOMATO COULIS

Gently warmed, sieved tomatoes with a hint of garlic and basil make a good accompaniment for all kinds of vegetarian dishes - stuffed aubergine, nut roast, baked red peppers as well as fish and chicken.

❖ Put the tomatoes in a pan, cover with water and bring to the boil. The moment the water starts to boil, remove the pan from the heat and leave the tomatoes in the hot water for 5 minutes.

❖ Then, carefully remove the tomatoes with a large draining spoon and, when cool enough, cut into quarters. Sieve using the rough side of the fine screen into the Bowl.

❖ Heat the olive oil and garlic over a very low heat, in order to infuse the flavours rather than cook the garlic. Stir in the sifted tomato, sugar and basil then season to taste with salt and black pepper.

❖ Warm gently just before serving, but take care not to overheat in order to preserve the beautiful fresh flavour.

6 tomatoes
water, for cooking
30ml (2 tbsp) olive oil
1 clove garlic, peeled and crushed
2.5ml (½ tsp) sugar
10 basil leaves, shredded
salt and freshly milled black pepper

✿ *Serves 2*
✗ *Not suitable for freezing*

SUMMER FRUITS IN A RASPBERRY COULIS

❖ Place both screens together, the fine one underneath the coarse one, rough side uppermost, in the bowl carrier and place in position on the Kenwood Bowl, then sieve the raspberries. This produces a very fine purée while removing all the tiny seeds of the berries.

❖ Stir the icing sugar and lemon juice into the puréed raspberry.

❖ Before serving, place the prepared fruits in a bowl and pour the Raspberry Coulis over the top. Alternatively the coulis can be used as a sauce for ice cream or pastries.

250g (9oz) raspberries, fresh or frozen
15-30ml (1-2 tbsp) icing sugar
5ml (1 tsp) lemon juice
450g (1 lb) fresh fruits, such as strawberries, peaches, raspberries, washed and cut

✿ *Serves 4*
✗ *Not suitable for freezing*

Banoffi & Ice Cream Pie

A base of crushed biscuits topped with sliced bananas and a thick layer of soft banana toffee. Served with scoops of vanilla ice cream, this pudding is easy to make and tastes divine.

1 x 400g (14oz) can sweetened condensed milk

water, for cooking

225g (8oz) digestive or sweetmeal biscuits

100g (4oz, ½ cup) butter, melted

3 large bananas

1 litre (1¼ pints) vanilla ice cream, the soft scoop variety

✪ *Serves 6*

✗ *Not suitable for freezing*

❖ Place the unopened can of sweetened condensed milk in a pan, cover with water and bring to the boil. Cover, reduce the heat and simmer gently for 2 hours. Leave in the pan to cool (this can be done a day in advance).

❖ Sieve the biscuits, using the rough side of the coarse screen, then stir in the butter until all the crumbs are coated. Tip into a large serving dish and flatten with the back of a spoon to make a base.

❖ Shake out the remaining crumbs from the screen then sieve one of the bananas into the Kenwood Bowl.

❖ Open the cooled can of condensed milk which will now have turned to soft toffee. Empty the can into the Kenwood Bowl and, using the K Beater at minimum speed, combine with the puréed banana.

❖ Peel and slice the remaining bananas and lay the slices on the biscuit crumb base. Spread the banana toffee over the top, cover with plastic film and refrigerate until required. This pudding will keep for up to 2 days.

❖ To serve, simply pile the ice cream on top of the toffee and let everyone help themselves.

Clockwise, from top left:

Fresh Tomato Coulis

Celeriac Purée

Winter Vegetable Soup

Summer Fruits in a Raspberry Coulis

Peeling Potatoes - the Easy Way

Potatoes and other root vegetables are healthy and nutritious, offering a low fat, high carbohydrate accompaniment, or even a main course dish in themselves. The preparation of these vegetables, though, must surely be the most odious task in the kitchen, unless you are fortunate to possess a machine designed for this purpose.

My first introduction to mechanical potato peeling was when I offered to help out with the cooking at a school camp. A sack of potatoes were cleaned, peeled and set to boil in no time at all, using the industrial Potato Peeler. It was as effortless as preparing potatoes at home for four people- not fifty.

It was some years, and many potatoes, later when I discovered that the Potato Peeler gives those same great results. Fortunately it has been designed for the domestic market and is more compact than the one I was using which would have taken up a huge space in even the largest kitchen.

The Potato Peeler will peel not only potatoes but also other root vegetables such as swedes, carrots and turnips. As it removes only the slightest amount of skin, the rich fibre and nutrients are retained in the vegetable.

Hints & Tips

❖ For Jacket Potatoes, use the Potato Peeler to simply clean the vegetables - switch on for a few minutes until the mud has been washed off.

❖ Best results are achieved by not over-filling the attachment, but peeling the vegetables in batches, adding enough water to cover the base plate.

❖ Make sure the potatoes or vegetables are all roughly the same size. If not chop them into evenly-sized pieces.

❖ Use the Potato Peeler between speeds 2 to 3.

SAUSAGE & POTATO CASSEROLE

This makes a really delightful meal for a family supper. It can be made in advance and heated through when needed, which also helps the flavours to develop.

❖ Preheat the oven and use the Potato Peeler to just clean the potatoes without peeling them completely. Thickly slice the sausages and layer them, with the onion, at the base of an ovenproof casserole or baking dish.

❖ Thinly slice the cleaned potatoes and spread them in a layer over the onion and sausage slices, together with the garlic and a sprinkling of salt and black pepper.

❖ Pour in the stock and then sprinkle the olive oil over the top. Cover the dish and bake for 1 hour. Remove the cover and bake for a further 15 minutes until the top has browned.

❖ Dice the peppers and sprinkle them over the top just before serving.

675g (1½ lb) potatoes
8 sausages, good quality
1 onion, finely sliced
1 clove garlic, crushed
salt and freshly milled black pepper
300ml (½ pint, 1¼ cups) chicken or vegetable stock
30ml (2 tbsp) olive oil
½ red pepper, deseeded and cored
½ green pepper, deseeded and cored

☐ *Oven Temperature 180°C (350°F, gas mark 4)*
✵ *Serves 4*
✗ *Not suitable for freezing*

GLAZED POTATO, TURNIP & CARROT BALLS

The Potato Peeler cleans not only potatoes but also a great variety of root vegetables. This dish is an excellent accompaniment to chicken, lamb, and many other meat dishes.

❖ Cut the carrots into 4 cm (1½") lengths. Cut the potatoes and turnip into pieces roughly the same size as the carrots.

❖ Place these pieces in the Potato Peeler, half covering them with water, and peel until they become rounded, in the shape of balls.

❖ Heat the butter in a pan and gently sauté the onion for 5 minutes until soft, but not coloured.

❖ Remove the carrot balls from the Potato Peeler and rinse before adding to the onion in the pan. Add the stock , bay leaves, salt and black pepper. Cover and simmer very gently for 5 minutes.

❖ Rinse the potato and turnip balls in water then add to the pan. Cover and barely simmer for a further 10 minutes or until the vegetables are almost cooked. Remove the lid and simmer for a further 5 minutes to glaze. Serve hot.

2 carrots
450g (1lb) potatoes
1 turnip, the size of an orange
10g (½oz) butter
½ onion, peeled and finely chopped
150ml (¼ pint, ½ cup) chicken or vegetable stock
2 bay leaves
salt and freshly milled black pepper

✵ *Serves 4*
✗ *Not suitable for freezing*

FLUFFY SPANISH POTATOES

900g (2lb) potatoes
60ml (4 tbsp) olive oil
salt and freshly milled black pepper
2 cloves garlic, crushed

☐ *Oven Temperature 190°C (375°F, gas mark 5)*
✗ *Not suitable for freezing*

❖ Cut the potatoes into 4cm (1½") cubes and place them in the Potato Peeler.

❖ Peel until the potatoes become rounded with a fluffy texture.

❖ Heat the olive oil in a roasting tray in the oven. Rinse and dry the potato balls then spoon them into the roasting tray, making sure they are well-coated with the hot oil.

❖ Season liberally with salt and black pepper then bake for 30 minutes until well cooked and golden. Sprinkle with the garlic and bake for a further 5 minutes. Serve immediately.

LUXURY POTATO SALAD

This is a large salad which will serve about 8 people for a buffet-style lunch. The Potato Peeler is used not to peel the potatoes but to clean them, leaving the vitamin-rich peel intact.

1.4kg (3lb) new potatoes
water, for cooking
30ml (2 tbsp) salt
fresh mint, optional
large onion, Spanish if possible
150ml (¼ pint, ½ cup) olive oil
30ml (1fl oz, ⅛ cup) white wine vinegar
150ml (¼ pint, ½ cup) mayonnaise
5ml (1 tsp) French mustard
5ml (1 tsp) sugar
30ml (2 tbsp) fresh parsley, chopped
30ml (2 tbsp) fresh chives, chopped
salt and freshly milled black pepper

❁ *Serves 8*
✗ *Not suitable for freezing*

❖ Use the Potato Peeler to just clean the potatoes – don't allow it to get to the peeling stage.

❖ Place the potatoes in a large pan and cover with cold water. Add the salt and bring slowly to the boil. If you have fresh mint add some to the pan.

❖ Cover and simmer gently for 20 minutes or until the potatoes are perfectly cooked, but not too soft (this will depend on their size).

❖ Meanwhile, finely chop the onion and mix it with the remaining ingredients to make a dressing. Season the dressing generously with salt and add a sprinkle of black pepper.

❖ When the potatoes are cooked, drain off the water and, as soon as they are cool enough to handle, halve and slice them.

❖ Place a layer of the potatoes in a serving bowl, then pour a little of the dressing over the top. Continue layering the potatoes with the dressing. Avoid stirring the potatoes as they are very delicate when warm and tend to break up easily. Taste as you go to ensure you have seasoned the dish adequately.

❖ Serve warm or cold with cooked meats or use as a buffet dish.

Clockwise, from top:

Luxury Potato Salad

Fluffy Spanish Potatoes

*Glazed Potato, Turnip
& Carrot Balls*

*Sausage & Potato
Casserole*

BACK TO THE GRINDSTONE - FLOUR MILLING AT HOME

You would imagine that with our more advanced farming practices and a better understanding of food production around the world our intake of basic grains would increase in variety. Alas, it seems to be quite the reverse - many of us are surviving more and more on a diet of wheat or rice, ignoring all those hundreds of grains and pulses which are available internationally.

In the processing of wheat, much of the outer bran layer and the wheat germ, so vital for minerals and vitamins, is removed. We spray our crops with poisons, genetically engineer tougher, more germ-resistant grains and then we are surprised how an increasing number of us are becoming allergic to such an integral part of our diet.

The Grain Mill offers a way of using a number of different and interesting grains and pulses while ensuring they retain the vital nutrients so important for a healthy diet. The attachment uses an authentic milling action to quickly and efficiently mill grains to a range of textures, from coarse to very fine flour. Brown rice, aduki beans, barley, lentils, spelt wheat are but a few examples of many grains and pulses which can be milled in the Grain Mill.

For those people who have an allergy it can be reassuring to mill flour at home, as this is the only way to really be sure of the initial quality of the grain. It also means that people with a gluten allergy can make alternative flours for recipes they could not otherwise eat. If you have an allergic reaction to gluten, do consult a doctor before introducing any new grains to your diet. The recipes in this section indicate whether or not they are gluten free.

HINTS & TIPS

❖ The internal parts of the Grain Mill should not be immersed in water. To clean, shake the loose grains free from the tube or take the pieces apart and brush out any grains or flour left inside.

❖ Often, grains left in the scroll of the Grain Mill will prevent removal of the attachment for the Chef. To prevent this, simply make sure all the grains have been milled before detaching.

❖ Use the Grain Mill at maximum speed.

CURRIED CHICKEN FLAN WITH BROWN RICE PASTRY

For thousands of years rice has been the staple diet of the Far East. It is widely grown in Europe, Africa, America and Australasia where it is traditionally used to make a wide variety of noodles, dumplings, breads, cakes and desserts. Rice, brown or white, makes a really well-flavoured flour suitable as an alternative to wheat flour in gluten free diets. It is easily digested and can be especially useful for making your own baby food.

❖ Preheat the oven. Mill the rice in the Grain Mill, using the finest setting, straight into the Kenwood Bowl.

❖ Use the K Beater to mix the rice flour with 50g (2oz, ¼ cup) of the butter or margarine at minimum speed until it resembles breadcrumbs. Add enough water to make a soft pastry dough.

❖ Either roll out the pastry to line a 24cm (9½") flan tin or simply press the mixture into the tin using your fingers and the back of a spoon. Bake blind for 10 minutes, until the pastry is crisp but not coloured.

❖ Meanwhile, heat the remaining butter or margarine in a pan and sauté the onion and apple for 5 minutes. Add the curry powder and cook over a gentle heat for a further 2 minutes. Remove from the heat.

❖ Beat together the eggs, milk and salt with a fork and stir into the curried onion and apple.

❖ Spread the chicken and raisins over the base of the flan pastry and pour over the curry mixture. Bake for 25 minutes until set and golden. Serve hot or cold.

PASTRY:

100g (4oz, ⅔ cup) brown rice

75g (3oz, ⅓ cup) butter or margarine, at room temperature

water, for mixing

FILLING:

1 medium onion, finely sliced

1 dessert apple, peeled, cored and finely diced

15ml (1 tbsp) curry powder

2 eggs

150ml (¼ pint, ½ cup) milk

large pinch of salt

175g (6oz) chicken, cooked and chopped

10g (½ oz, ⅛ cup) raisins

☐ *Oven Temperature 190°C (375°F, gas mark 5)*

✿ *Serves 6*

✤ *Gluten free*

✳ *Suitable for freezing*

CHOCOLATE PUDDING

❖ Preheat the oven. Mill the rice in the Grain Mill using the finest setting.

❖ Gently heat the milk in a pan, then add the rice flour and bring to the boil, stirring constantly. Cook gently for 5 minutes, still stirring.

❖ Remove from the heat and add the sugar, vanilla essence and chocolate pieces, stirring until the chocolate has melted.

❖ Pour into a lightly oiled baking dish, approximately 20cm (8") in diameter, and bake for 30 minutes. Serve hot with a custard sauce or cream.

50g (2oz, ⅓ cup) brown rice

575ml (1 pint, 2¼ cups) milk

2oz (50g, ¼ cup) sugar

1.25ml (¼ tsp) vanilla essence

150g (5oz) plain chocolate pieces

☐ *Oven Temperature 190°C (375°F, gas mark 5)*

✿ *Serves 4-6*

✤ *Gluten free*

✗ *Not suitable for freezing*

SPELT FLOUR BREAD

Spelt is an ancient grain, dating back to Roman times, which was once widely used throughout Europe and Asia. It comes from the same family as wheat and imparts a lovely nutty flavour to breads and pastries. However, with farmers today preferring modern wheat grains which are easier to thresh, we have almost lost this ingredient. Although spelt grain contains gluten, many who suffer from a gluten allergy find they are able to tolerate this flour. If you happen to be allergic to gluten, do consult your doctor as a matter of course before introducing any new grains into your diet.

450g (1lb, 2⅔ cups) spelt grain

5ml (1 tsp) easy-blend yeast, (see p.30 for yeast conversion)

5ml (1 tsp) salt

30ml (2 tbsp) vegetable or olive oil

5ml (1 tsp) honey

400ml (14fl oz, 1¼ cups) warm water

☐ *Oven Temperature 190°C (375°F, gas mark 5)*
○ *Makes 1 medium loaf*
❀ *Not gluten free*
✳ *Suitable for freezing*

❖ Mill the spelt grain in the Grain Mill, using the finest setting, straight into the Kenwood Bowl.

❖ Add the remaining ingredients and use the Dough Hook at minimum speed to knead the dough for 5 minutes. The dough should be very soft and sticky, so do put in all the liquid.

❖ Remove the Bowl with the dough inside and cover it loosely with plastic film or a damp cloth. Leave to rise in a warm place for about 30-60 minutes until doubled in size.

❖ Preheat the oven then re-knead the dough for 1 minute. Put into a well oiled loaf tin. It will still be very sticky, so pat it down with the Spatula and a little spelt flour if necessary.

❖ Leave to rise again, uncovered, for 15–30 minutes in a warm place. When nicely puffed up, bake for 35 minutes or until the loaf sounds hollow when tapped on its base. Leave to cool on a wire rack.

BARLEY MALT LOAF

❖ Preheat the oven then oil and line the base of a small loaf tin.

❖ Mill the barley in the Grain Mill using the finest setting. Put the malt extract, golden syrup and butter or margarine into a pan and heat until the butter has melted.

❖ Place the barley flour and syrup mixture in the Kenwood Bowl. Add the remaining ingredients and mix together thoroughly using the K Beater at minimum speed.

❖ Spoon the mixture into the prepared loaf tin and cover with foil. Place this in a roasting tray then pour boiling water into the tray to a depth of 5 cm (2").

❖ Bake for 1 hour, then uncover the loaf and cook for a further 15-30 minutes, or until an inserted skewer comes out clean. Cool on a wire rack and serve sliced and buttered.

225g (8oz, 1¼ cups) pearl barley

75ml (5 tbsp) malt extract

90ml (6 tbsp) golden syrup, partially inverted sugar syrup

50g (2oz) butter or margarine

5 ml (1 tsp) baking powder

pinch of salt

100g (4oz, ⅔ cup) raisins

1 egg

90ml (6 tbsp) milk

boiling water, for cooking

☐ *Oven Temperature 160°C (325°F, gas mark 3)*

✪ *Serves 6*

❀ *Not gluten free*

✳ *Suitable for freezing*

OAT, HONEY & APPLE ROCK CAKES

❖ Mill the rolled oats in the Grain Mill, using the finest setting, straight into the Kenwood Bowl.

❖ Add the remaining ingredients and mix together using the K Beater at minimum speed. Spoon 12 mounds on to lightly oiled non-stick baking sheets, leaving a little space in between each mound.

❖ Bake for 20 minutes until golden. The outside should be crispy but the centre should be soft - this gives these cakes their charm!

150g (5oz, 1½ cups) rolled oats

2.5ml (½ tsp) bicarbonate of soda

pinch of salt

22.5ml (1½ tbsp) vegetable oil

50g (2oz, ¼ cup) raisins

60ml (4 tbsp) honey

2 small eating apples, cored and finely chopped

☐ *Oven Temperature 190°C (375°F, gas mark 5)*

◯ *Makes 12*

❀ *Not gluten free*

✳ *Suitable for freezing*

Date & Buckwheat Pudding

50g (2oz, ⅓ cup) buckwheat

575ml (1 pint, 2¼ cups) milk, dairy or soya

100g (4oz, ½ cup) sugar

2.5ml (½ tsp) vanilla essence

100g (4oz, ¼ cup) dates, chopped

☐ Oven Temperature 190°C (375°F, gas mark 5)

✪ Serves 4-6

✤ Gluten free

✗ Not suitable for freezing

❖ Preheat the oven and mill the buckwheat in the Grain Mill using the finest setting.

❖ Heat the milk until simmering and whisk in the buckwheat flour. Simmer gently for 5 minutes.

❖ Remove from the heat and add the sugar, vanilla essence and chopped dates, stirring to dissolve the sugar.

❖ Pour into a lightly oiled baking dish, approximately 2cm (8") in diameter, and bake for 40 minutes. Serve hot.

Grilled Millet & Parmesan Squares

These are really simple to make and are delicious served tossed in salad. They can be made in advance and grilled at the last minute.

150g (5oz, ¼ cup) millet

575ml (1 pint, 2¼ cups) chicken or vegetable stock

25g (1oz, ⅓ cup) Parmesan cheese, grated

✪ Serves 4

✤ Gluten free

✗ Not suitable for freezing

❖ Mill the millet in the Grain Mill using a medium setting.

❖ Place the millet flour and stock in a large, heavy-based pan and bring to simmering point, stirring continuously. Simmer for 15 minutes, still stirring, until the mixture becomes very thick.

❖ Add half the Parmesan cheese and stir until it has melted. Then pour into a square, lightly oiled tin, and allow to cool.

❖ When the mixture is cold it should be completely solid. Turn out on to a chopping board and cut into bite-sized squares. Place on a wire rack and sprinkle with the remaining cheese.

❖ Grill for 5 minutes then serve hot or cold with a salad.

THE ART OF COFFEE MAKING

The history of coffee begins in Aden in 1454, when a certain Sheik Gemaleddin fell ill. He called for the cherries of a wild native bush in Etheopia, where he had been exiled, and had the stones (coffee beans) crushed with animal fat and maize, to make a foodstuff for curing his illness. He found the food to be so successful that he recommended it to his monks to help them stay awake during their nightly vigil. It was later turned into a drink, and thus, coffee was discovered.

As coffee became popular more and more countries started cultivating it. The process takes 5 years, after which the ripe red cherries are picked by hand then sent to a processing plant for the stones to be removed and roasted. After roasting, the beans are open to oxidation and will stay good for 6 weeks. When ground, coffee will only last for 2 days, so storage is important. Home grinding is therefore the best way to produce fresh, aromatic coffee.

The Coffee Grinder uses the traditional method, two metal rollers which open up the cell structure of each bean to allow the full flavour to be released, which is far better than other methods which smash the beans.

An adjustable knob with 6 settings allows you to choose the degree of grinding required. The table below is a guide to settings for the more popular methods of coffee making.

METHOD	COARSENESS (SETTING)
Turkish/Greek Coffee	Fine (1)
Glass Balloon/Vacuum (Cona)	Fine to Medium Fine (1-2)
Filter/Drip	Fine to Medium (1-3)
Cafetière	Medium (3-4)
Percolator	Medium to Coarse (4-6)
Jug	Coarse (6)

HINTS & TIPS

❖ To ensure coffee beans stay at their best, store them in an airtight container and keep in a very cool place. They can even be frozen but defrost well before grinding.

❖ To clean, simply wipe the body with a cloth, do not immerse in water.

❖ The collecting dish is reversible for either 2 cups or a continuous flow.

❖ Use the Coffee Grinder between speeds 4 to 5.

MOCHA FINO

This coffee is rich, dark and luxurious.

❖ Grind the coffee beans in the Coffee Grinder using the appropriate setting (see page 116), then prepare the coffee with the boiling water, using a percolator or cafetière.

❖ Meanwhile, put the milk in a pan and heat to boiling point.

❖ Place the sugar, cocoa powder and cinnamon in a cup. Pour over the hot coffee, stirring well.

❖ Add the boiled milk then sprinkle grated chocolate over the top. Serve immediately.

45ml (3 tbsp) coffee beans
115ml (4fl oz, ½ cup) boiling water
115ml (4fl oz, ½ cup) milk
15ml (1 tbsp) sugar
1.25ml (¼ tsp) cocoa powder
1.25ml (¼ tsp) cinnamon
15ml (1 tbsp) dark semi-sweet chocolate, grated

○ Makes 1 cup
✗ Not suitable for freezing

TURKISH/GREEK COFFEE

Tradition dies hard when it comes to coffee making in Turkey or Greece - one of the merits which was essential for a good bride was her ability to master the art of coffee preparation under the scrutiny of her future mother-in-law. An important part of the process is the authentic coffee pot called a 'briki' or 'ibrik', which is made of finely beaten brass.

The coffee needs to be so finely ground that it almost becomes a powder, to produce a thick, strong coffee with a wonderfully frothy top. The Kenwood Coffee Grinder is able to produce ground coffee which will produce similar results.

❖ Grind the coffee beans in the Coffee Grinder using the finest setting.

❖ If you have a briki, use it – otherwise use a small pan.

❖ Place the coffee, sugar and water in the briki or pan and bring to the boil while stirring. When it starts to boil and becomes frothy, remove from the heat until the froth subsides.

❖ Return to a brisk heat and bring to the boil a second time until it becomes frothy again. Remove from the heat and repeat this process twice more.

❖ Stir in the rose water, if using, then pour into a warm jug or individual cups. Serve black.

15-20ml (1-1½ tbsp) coffee beans
5ml (1 tsp) sugar
150ml (¼ pint, ½ cup) water
few drops of rose water, optional

○ Makes 1 cup
✗ Not suitable for freezing

IRISH COFFEE

This authentic recipe from Ireland was sent to me with an accompanying message - "always add a drop more Irish whiskey for the fairies." In other words, the quantity of whiskey given is a rough guide - if you feel like adding more, do so!

30ml (2 tbsp) coffee beans
175ml (6fl oz, ⅔ cup) boiling water
45ml (3 tbsp) double cream
extra hot water
30ml (2 tbsp) Irish whiskey
12.5ml (2½ tsp) sugar
cocoa powder, for serving

○ *Makes 1 glass*
✗ *Not suitable for freezing*

❖ Grind the coffee beans in the Coffee Grinder using the appropriate setting (see page 116). Prepare the coffee with the boiling water, using a percolator or cafetière.

❖ Whip the cream lightly (you can use the Balloon Whisk for this) until it becomes thick and can almost hold its shape.

❖ Meanwhile, heat a glass with some hot water, placing a metal teaspoon inside to prevent the glass from cracking. Leave for 1 minute then pour out the water.

❖ Pour the hot coffee into the glass, with the teaspoon still in place, then add the whiskey and sugar, stirring well to dissolve the sugar.

❖ Hold a teaspoon so that the base is just touching the surface of the coffee. Then carefully pour the cream into it so that the cream floats onto the coffee to form a layer.

❖ Dust the top with cocoa powder, place on a saucer and serve.

PEPPERMINT COFFEE CRÈME

30ml (2 tbsp) coffee beans
175ml (6fl oz, ⅔ cup) boiling water
extra hot water
15ml (1 tbsp) Crème de Menthe, peppermint liqueur
5ml (1 tsp) sugar
45ml (3 tbsp) double cream

○ *Makes 1 glass*
✗ *Not suitable for freezing*

❖ Grind the coffee beans in the Coffee Grinder using the appropriate setting (see page 116). Prepare the coffee with the boiling water, using a percolator or cafetière.

❖ Whip the double cream lightly (you can use the Balloon Whisk for this) until it becomes thick and can almost hold its shape.

❖ Meanwhile, heat a glass with some hot water, placing a metal teaspoon inside to prevent the glass from cracking. Leave for 1 minute then pour the water out.

❖ Pour the hot coffee into the glass, with the teaspoon still in place, then add the Crème de Menthe and sugar, stirring well to dissolve the sugar.

❖ Hold a teaspoon so that the base is just touching the surface of the coffee. Carefully pour the cream into it so that the cream floats onto the coffee to form a layer. Place the glass on a saucer to serve.

Dark Roasted Coffee Beans

Fresh Home-made Cream

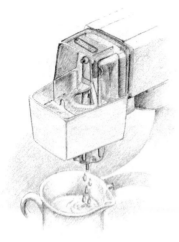

Making cream from butter and milk is not exactly fundamental cookery, but more a clever piece of technology created by Kenwood for those of us who run out of cream just before serving dessert at dinner, or for those who live in countries where fresh cream is a hard-to-come-by luxury. With the Cream Maker, as long as there is butter and milk, you will always be able to make fresh home-made cream. It is quick and easy to prepare, whips and looks the same and tastes identical.

It is an amazing process - reconstituting butter with a liquid to make cream. By making butter (see recipe on page 41) from double cream and then transforming it back again we can learn so much about two ingredients which have become so elementary to much of the world's cookery.

Cream is different from one country to the next. France uses Crème Fraîche, Italy uses Mascarpone cream cheese and America, heavy and light cream. The Cream Maker, however, can bring a uniformity which is sometimes needed in international cookery.

Below is a basic method which you can use for the following recipes.

Hints & Tips

❖ Reconstituted dried milk can be used as an alternative to fresh, as well as low fat milks.

❖ Be careful not to overheat the milk and butter - the mixture needs only to be warm.

Basic Cream Recipe

Double/Heavy Cream:

175ml (6fl oz, ⅔ cup) milk
175g (6oz, ¾ cup) unsalted butter

Single/Light Cream:

225ml (8fl oz, 1 cup) milk
100g (4oz, ½ cup) unsalted butter

○ *Makes 1 quantity, 300ml*
(½ pint, 1¼ cups)
✗ *Not suitable for freezing*

❖ Warm the milk and butter gently in a pan, until the butter has melted.

❖ Attach the Cream Maker to the Chef, place a dish or bowl underneath and switch to speed 3.

❖ Stir the warm milk mixture before pouring it into the Cream Maker.

❖ Leave the fresh cream to cool before using. If it is to be whipped, chill well in the refrigerator for at least 8 hours then whip using the Balloon Whisk.

SOURED CREAM, BLUE CHEESE & CHIVE DIP

❖ Mix together the Double Cream and lemon juice and put to one side.

❖ Pound together the garlic and salt in a pestle and mortar. Add the mustard powder and a third of the cream mixture. Crumble in the blue cheese then stir with a fork, or blend in the Multi Mill, to make as smooth a paste as possible.

❖ Stir the chives and the remaining cream mixture into the cheese paste, then season to taste with salt and black pepper. Serve in a bowl surrounded by savoury biscuits, potato chips or vegetable sticks for dipping.

1 quantity of Double Cream (see p.120 for preparation)

15ml (1 tbsp) lemon juice

1 small clove garlic, peeled

1.25ml (¼ tsp) salt

2.5ml (½ tsp) mustard powder

50g (2oz, ⅓ cup) blue cheese

45ml (3 tbsp) fresh chives, finely chopped

salt and freshly milled black pepper

✪ *Serves 8 as a starter or snack*
✗ *Not suitable for freezing*

CREAM OF COURGETTE & SPINACH SOUP

❖ Heat the oil in a pan and gently sauté the onion and courgette for 5 minutes until soft and transparent.

❖ Add the potato, spinach and stock. Bring to the boil and simmer for 20 minutes.

❖ Cool a little before blending until smooth in the Liquidiser.

❖ Return to the pan, stir in the Single Cream, reserving a little for serving, and taste before seasoning with salt and black pepper. Warm through without boiling so as not to spoil the flavour of the soup.

❖ Just before serving, sprinkle with the chopped chives and a swirl of cream.

30ml (2 tbsp) vegetable oil

1 medium onion, peeled and chopped

1 large courgette, chopped

1 medium potato, peeled and chopped

100g (4oz) spinach, washed thoroughly

1.25 litres (2 pints, 4 ½ cups) chicken or vegetable stock

1 quantity of Single Cream (see p.120 for preparation)

salt and freshly milled black pepper

30ml (2 tbsp) fresh chives, finely chopped

✪ *Serves 4*
✗ *Not suitable for freezing*

LEMON & RASPBERRY POSSET

This is definitely my favourite pudding - it is light and refreshing, but also rich and luxurious.

2 lemons, washed
2 quantities of Double Cream
(see p.120 for preparation)
85g (3½ oz, ½ cup) caster sugar
225g (8oz) raspberries

❂ *Serves 4*
✗ *Not suitable for freezing*

❖ Finely grate the zest from the lemons and put to one side. Then extract the juice (using the Citrus Juicer if you wish) and leave that to one side. Place the lemon zest, Double Cream and caster sugar in a pan and bring to the boil.

❖ Pour the lemon juice into a bowl large enough to hold the cream mixture. When the cream mixture just reaches the boil pour on to the lemon juice in the bowl. Stir well then refrigerate for 30 minutes.

❖ Meanwhile, divide the raspberries between 4 ramekins or tall glasses and chill. Divide the cream mixture between each of the chilled glasses, cover with plastic film and refrigerate for at least 2 hours, or preferably overnight.

FRESH FRUIT WITH CRÈME FOUETTÉE

Desserts don't always need to be complicated to be delectable!

2 quantities of Double Cream,
well chilled (see p.120 for
preparation)
50g (2oz, ¼ cup) caster sugar
2.5ml (½ tsp) vanilla essence
450g (1 lb) fresh fruits such as
strawberries or raspberries

❂ *Serves 4*
✗ *Not suitable for freezing*

❖ Place the Double Cream, sugar and vanilla essence in the Kenwood Bowl and use the Balloon Whisk at speed 5 to whisk the cream until it thickens to the soft peak stage.

❖ Place the fresh fruit in 4 tall glasses and spoon the cream mixture over the top. Chill again before serving.

Fresh Fruit with
Crème Fouettée

BISCUITS WITH A BITE, COOKIES WITH A CRUNCH

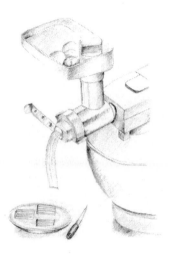

During Roman times, housewives developed a method of baking small flat cakes, removing them from their tins and then returning them to the oven to dry and become hard. These cakes became known as 'Reims Biscuits' and, for many centuries, became the staple food of soldiers and sailors, due to their ability to be stored for long periods of time. Pliny once said that they would keep for centuries.

The word biscuit actually comes from the French words 'bis' – meaning twice, and 'cuit' – meaning cooked, though nowadays they are usually baked only once. Cookie is a term used more in America but symbolises the same type of confection.

Biscuits have served not only to keep military men's hunger pangs at bay but have also been the life force of others. From a healthy angle, it has also been known for biscuits and cookies to be enriched with vitamins and distributed to children. Explorer, Chateaubri, in his record of adventures to the New World wrote about how, reduced to a solitary existence, he dined on ships biscuits, a little sugar and lemon.

The Cookie Maker Adaptor is the key to simple and quick home-baked cookies which are always far more wholesome and delicious than the dry, ready-bought variety. There is a choice of 4 different shapes through which to extrude the dough, each one producing a different result. Cookie making is great fun for children who adore getting involved with anything that tastes scrumptious at the end. The following recipes are a suggestion of what can be done using the Cookie Maker Adaptor and might give an insight into how cookie manufacturers can produce so many perfect and evenly-sized cookies.

HINTS & TIPS

❖ Lining baking sheets with parchment or other non-stick baking paper makes removing cookies and biscuits very simple.

❖ Always leave space between the cookies on the baking sheets, as the unbaked mixture tends to spread when it is in the oven.

❖ Use the Cookie Maker Adaptor at speed 4. This can be increased as you become more adept at cookie making.

CHOCOLATE DREAMS

❖ Preheat the oven and have ready some non-stick baking sheets or baking sheets either lightly oiled or lined with parchment.

❖ Use the K Beater at speed 3 to cream together the butter and sugar. Add the egg and beat until smooth. You may need to stop the Chef once to scrape the mixture down into the Bowl, using the Spatula. Sift in the flour, cocoa powder, baking powder and salt and continue mixing at minimum speed until a dough has formed.

❖ Fit the Cookie Maker Adaptor to the Mincer attachment on the Chef and select the flat ridged shape. Pull off pieces of biscuit dough in sausage shapes and feed into the Mincer tube. Cut the biscuits to a length of about 5 cm (2").

❖ Place the cookies, ridged side uppermost, on the baking sheets and sprinkle with caster sugar. Bake for 10 minutes then remove from the oven and leave to cool on a wire rack.

❖ To make the filling, heat the cream in a pan over a low heat and then stir in the chocolate. When the chocolate has melted, pour the mixture into the Kenwood Bowl and, when cool, whisk at maximum speed until fluffy.

❖ Sandwich the cookies together in pairs, ridged side outermost, using a spoonful of the filling. Store in an airtight container.

COOKIES:

100g (4oz, ½ cup) butter, at room temperature
50g (2oz, ¼ cup) caster sugar
1 egg
200g (7oz, 1½ cups) plain flour
25g (1oz, ¼ cup) cocoa powder
2.5ml (½ tsp) baking powder
pinch of salt
extra caster sugar, for decorating

FILLING:

85ml (3fl oz, ⅓ cup) double cream
75g (3oz) plain chocolate, broken into pieces

☐ *Oven Temperature 180°C (350°F, gas mark 4)*
○ *Makes 30 cookies*
✗ *Not suitable for freezing*

JAMAICAN CRUNCHIES

❖ Preheat the oven and have ready some non-stick baking sheets or baking sheets either lightly oiled or lined with parchment.

❖ Use the K Beater at minimum speed to cream together the butter and brown sugar. Add the rum, flour, salt and coconut milk powder and mix until smooth.

❖ Fit the Cookie Maker Adaptor to the Mincer attachment on the Chef and select the large star shape. Pull off pieces of biscuit dough in sausage shapes and feed into the Mincer tube. Cut at 8cm (3") intervals and mould into shapes.

❖ Place on the baking sheets and sprinkle with desiccated coconut.

❖ Bake for 8-10 minutes until barely coloured, then leave to cool slightly before transferring to a wire rack.

225g (8oz, 1 cup) butter, at room temperature
175g (6oz, 1 cup) brown sugar
20ml (4 tsp) dark rum
200g (7oz, 1¼ cups) plain flour
pinch of salt
75g (3oz, ¼ cup) coconut milk powder
50g (2oz, ⅔ cup) desiccated coconut

☐ *Oven Temperature 180°C (350°F, gas mark 4)*
○ *Makes 30 cookies*
✗ *Not suitable for freezing*

HONEY & LEMON CREAMS

COOKIES:

225g (8oz, 1¾ cups) self raising flour

50g (2oz, ¼ cup) caster sugar

100g (4oz, ½ cup) butter, at room temperature

100g (4oz, ⅓ cup) clear honey

FILLING:

50g (2oz, ¼ cup) butter, at room temperature

100g (4oz, 1 cup) icing sugar, sifted

zest of 1 lemon, finely grated

15ml (1 tbsp) lemon juice

☐ *Oven Temperature 200°C (400°F, gas mark 6)*

○ *Makes 40 cookies*

✗ *Not suitable for freezing*

❖ Preheat the oven and have ready some non-stick baking sheets or baking sheets either lightly oiled or lined with parchment.

❖ Put the flour and sugar into the Kenwood Bowl. Add the butter and use the K Beater at speed 1 to produce a mixture resembling breadcrumbs. Pour on the honey and mix until a dough is formed.

❖ Fit the Cookie Maker Adaptor to the Mincer attachment on the Chef and select the flat ridged shape. Pull off pieces of cookie dough in sausage shapes and feed into the Mincer tube. Cut at 5cm (2") intervals.

❖ Place the biscuits on the baking sheets, leaving a little space in between each, then bake for 4 minutes until golden. Leave to cool a little before transferring to a wire rack.

❖ To make the lemon filling, use the K Beater at speed 1 to beat together the butter, icing sugar, lemon zest and lemon juice.

❖ Sandwich the cookies together in pairs, ridged side outermost, using a spoonful of the lemon filling.

VIENNESE FINGERS

225g (8oz, 1 cup) butter, at room temperature

50g (2oz, ½ cup) icing sugar, sifted

2.5ml (½ tsp) vanilla essence

225g (8oz, 1¾ cups) plain flour

pinch of salt

75g (3oz) plain chocolate, broken into pieces

☐ *Oven Temperature 180°C (350°F, gas mark 4)*

○ *Makes 24 cookies*

✗ *Not suitable for freezing*

❖ Preheat the oven and have ready some non-stick baking sheets or baking sheets either lightly oiled or lined with parchment.

❖ Use the K Beater at speed 1 to beat together the butter and icing sugar until light and fluffy. Then add in the vanilla essence.

❖ Sift the flour and salt into the Bowl and continue mixing with the K Beater at a low speed until a dough is formed.

❖ Fit the Cookie Maker Adaptor to the Mincer attachment on the Chef and select the large star shape. Pull off pieces of cookie dough in sausage shapes and feed into the Mincer tube. Cut at 8cm (3") intervals to form finger shapes.

❖ Place the cookies on the baking sheets, leaving a little space in between each one. Bake for 10 minutes until lightly coloured, then transfer to a wire rack to cool.

❖ Put the chocolate into a bowl and place over a pan of barely simmering water. Stir until melted. Dip the ends of the cookies into the melted chocolate and place on a wire rack to harden.

KOURAMBIETHES

A wonderful Greek shortbread, this recipe is from one of my favourite cookery books, 'Under the Influence of Bright Sunbeams', written by the Countess China de Burnay in which she looks at centuries of natural cuisine. The shortbread is much easier to make thanks to the help of the Cookie Maker Adaptor.

❖ Preheat the oven and have ready some non-stick baking sheets or baking sheets either lightly oiled or lined with parchment.

❖ Use the K Beater at minimum speed to cream together the butter, sugar and ground saffron. Add the egg yolks, Ouzo and ground almonds and continue to mix until smooth.

❖ Sift in the cornflour and plain flour and mix, using the K Beater at speed 1, until a dough has formed. You may have to scrape the Bowl around once with the Spatula to ensure an even mixing.

❖ Fit the Cookie Maker Adaptor to the Mincer attachment on the Chef and select the large star shape. Pull off pieces of biscuit dough in sausage shapes and feed into the Mincer tube. Cut at 8cm (3") intervals and bend to form a horseshoe shape.

❖ Place on the baking sheets and bake for 15 minutes until lightly golden. Leave to cool for a few minutes before transferring to a wire rack.

❖ When completely cool, brush lightly with the orange flower water and dip into icing sugar. Keep in an airtight container.

225g (8oz, 1 cup) butter, at room temperature

225g (8oz, 1 cup) caster sugar

2.5ml (½ tsp) ground saffron

2 egg yolks

15ml (1 tbsp) Ouzo aniseed-flavoured spirit

175g (6oz, 1½ cups) ground almonds

75g (3oz, ½ cup) cornflour

250g (9oz, 2 cups) plain white flour

orange flower water and icing sugar, for decorating

☐ Oven Temperature 180°C (350°F, gas mark 4)

◯ Makes 50 cookies

✗ Not suitable for freezing

CHEESE & CHILLI STICKS

❖ Preheat the oven and have ready some non-stick baking sheets or baking sheets either lightly oiled or lined with parchment.

❖ Place the flour, salt, baking powder and butter in the Kenwood Bowl and mix with the K Beater at minimum speed until the mixture resembles breadcrumbs.

❖ Add the cheese and chilli powder and continue mixing until well combined. Add the egg and mix until a smooth dough has formed.

❖ Fit the Cookie Maker Adaptor to the Mincer attachment on the Chef and select the small circle shape. Pull off pieces of biscuit dough in sausage shapes and feed into the Mincer tube. Cut at 13cm (5") intervals.

❖ Place on the baking sheets and bake for 8-10 minutes. Leave to cool slightly before transferring to a wire rack.

175g (6oz, 1⅓ cups) plain flour

pinch of salt

7.5ml (1½ tsp) baking powder

75g (3oz, ⅓ cup) butter, at room temperature

50g (2oz, ⅔ cup) cheese such as Cheddar or Emmental, grated

2.5ml (½ tsp) chilli powder

1 egg

☐ Oven Temperature 180°C (350°F, gas mark 4)

◯ Makes 30 cookies

✗ Not suitable for freezing

MOCHA TRIANGLES

325g (12oz, 1½ cups) butter, at room temperature

325g (12oz, 1⅓ cups) caster sugar

1 egg

5ml (1 tsp) vanilla essence

425g (15oz, 3½ cups) plain flour

salt

10ml (2 tsp) instant coffee, dissolved in 15ml (1 tbsp) hot water

25g (1oz, ¼ cup) cocoa powder

5ml (1 tsp) almond essence

□ *Oven Temperature 180°C (350°F, gas mark 4)*

○ *Makes 80 cookies*

✗ *Not suitable for freezing*

❖ Use the K Beater at minimum speed to cream together the butter and sugar until fluffy. Add the egg and beat until smooth.

❖ Divide the mixture into three, leaving one third in the Kenwood Bowl.

❖ To the mixture in the bowl add the vanilla essence, a third of the flour and a pinch of salt. Mix at minimum speed until smooth then remove the mixture from the Bowl, scraping away as much as you can with the Spatula.

❖ Put a second third of the mixture into the Bowl and add to this the coffee, half the remaining flour and a pinch of salt. Mix gently until it has formed a smooth dough then remove the dough, again scraping the Bowl clean with the Spatula.

❖ Put the last third of the original mixture into the Bowl and add to this the cocoa powder, almond essence, the remaining flour and a pinch of salt. Mix until smooth. You will now have 3 different coloured balls of dough.

❖ Fit the Cookie Maker Adaptor to the Mincer attachment on the Chef and select the small circle shape. Pull off pieces of dough in sausage shapes from one of the coloured balls and feed into the Mincer tube. Repeat with each of the other two balls of dough, cleaning the attachment, if necessary, in between. Cut off the pipes of biscuit at about 30cm (12") intervals.

❖ Lay a sheet of plastic film about 40cm (16") long on the work surface. Lay 6 coloured pipes on the plastic film next to each other. Lay more pipes on top, trying not to have two of the same colour together. Stack so that you end up with a triangle of pipes when viewed from the end. Wrap the plastic film around the cookie dough and gently push the pipes firmly together.

❖ Refrigerate the mixture for at least 2 hours so that it becomes firm.

❖ Preheat the oven and have ready some non-stick baking sheets or baking sheets either lightly oiled or lined with parchment. Unwrap the dough, slice into even pieces, about 2.5mm (⅒") thick, and place on the baking sheets. Bake for 5 minutes, then transfer to a wire rack to cool.

GRATING - FOR FINER RESULTS

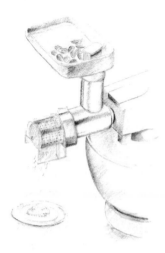

Nowadays, so many ingredients can easily be bought ready-grated. Though this may be convenient, it can affect the flavour of the food and is often a more expensive choice. Freshly grated nuts have an aroma and texture which is infinitely better than the ready-ground varieties, and the difference to the flavour of the resulting dish is immense.

Cheese is another good example of where it pays to grate fresh - especially Parmesan which can be almost a tasteless powder when it is bought in its processed form.

Many cooks can be tempted to use ready-grated food as grating by hand can be a real bore, and all too often the small quantity does not warrant the use of a large implement. This is where the Fine Grater comes in handy. It is a compact adaptor which attaches to the Mincer attachment. It evenly grates nuts, chocolate, Parmesan cheese, some vegetables, fudge and many other types of food.

The main use for the Fine Grater Adaptor, especially in countries like Austria, is for grinding almonds. It really produces such a fine, almost powdery, texture of almonds which is so important in cooking, and is also a far more economical method of obtaining this ingredient.

Ground almonds have multiple uses in cakes and cookies, sweet and savoury dishes alike, and also make an excellent alternative to flour for thickening sauces and soups.

HINTS & TIPS

❖ Leave the Chef running for a while after the last ingredients have been fed through to allow time for every last piece of food to be grated.

❖ As well as its main ingredient, almonds, the Fine Grater can be used for potatoes, and for making pasta noodles for clear soups.

WALNUT, ALMOND & HAZELNUT BISCUITS

This recipe has been adapted from my favourite cookery book 'Under the Influence of Bright Sunbeams', by the Countess China de Burnay.

❖ Preheat the oven. Fit the Fine Grater Adaptor to the Mincer attachment on the Chef, then grate the hazelnuts into a bowl.

❖ Put the egg yolks, sugar, orange and vanilla essence into the Kenwood Bowl and use the K Beater at speed 1 to cream them together.

❖ Add the chopped walnuts, grated hazelnuts and orange zest.

❖ Line a baking sheet with parchment and spoon small amounts of the mixture onto the prepared sheet. There should be enough mixture for about 20 biscuits.

❖ Sprinkle the flaked almonds over the biscuits and bake for 18-20 minutes, until just golden. Leave to cool on the baking sheet, then store in an airtight container.

100g (4oz, 1⅓ cups) hazelnuts
5 egg yolks
100g (4oz, ½ cup) caster sugar
2.5ml (½ tsp) orange essence
2.5ml (½ tsp) vanilla essence
50g (2oz, ⅖ cup) chopped walnuts
zest of 1 orange, finely grated
50g (2oz, ⅖ cup) flaked almonds

☐ *Oven Temperature 150°C (300°F, gas mark 2)*
○ *Makes 20 biscuits*
✗ *Not suitable for freezing*

ALMOND FUDGE CRUMBLES

❖ Preheat the oven. Fit the Fine Grater Adaptor to the Mincer attachment on the Chef, then grate the almonds and the pieces of fudge alternately so that the almonds help to push the fudge through the attachment. Collect the gratings in a bowl.

❖ Mix together the flour, bicarbonate of soda and the butter using the K Beater at speed 1 until the mixture resembles breadcrumbs.

❖ Add the sugar, egg, almond essence, grated almonds and fudge then continue mixing to form a dough. Pat into the shape of a log about 23cm (9") long. Cut into 24 slices and place on non-stick, lightly oiled baking sheets, leaving a gap in between each slice. Sprinkle with the flaked almonds and bake for 12 minutes. Leave to cool on the baking sheet.

75g (3oz, ½ cup) blanched almonds
75g (3oz) vanilla fudge, in pieces
200g (7oz, 1½ cups) plain flour
2.5ml (½ tsp) bicarbonate of soda
100g (4oz, ½ cup) butter, at room temperature
100g (4oz, ⅖ cup) brown sugar
1 egg
2.5ml (½ tsp) almond essence
25 g (1 oz, ⅓ cup) flaked almonds

☐ *Oven Temperature 190°C (375°F, gas mark 5)*
○ *Makes 24 biscuits*
✗ *Not suitable for freezing*

HAZELNUT & WHITE CHOCOLATE BROWNIES

250g (9oz) white chocolate

50g (2oz, ¼ cup) butter, melted

2 eggs

75g (3oz, ⅓ cup) caster sugar

100g (4oz, 1⅓ cups) shelled
hazelnuts, roughly chopped

pinch of salt

5ml (1 tsp) vanilla essence

75g (3oz, ¾ cup) self raising flour

☐ *Oven Temperature 180°C
(325°F, gas mark 4)*

◯ *Makes 16 brownies*

✗ *Not suitable for freezing*

❖ Preheat the oven, then oil and line the base of a 22cm (9") square baking tin which is at least 5cm (2") deep.

❖ Fit the Fine Grater Adaptor to the Mincer attachment on the Chef then grate the white chocolate into the Kenwood Bowl.

❖ Add the melted butter, eggs, sugar, chopped hazelnuts, salt and vanilla essence, then mix with the K Beater at speed 1, until the mixture is smooth. Add the flour and mix to combine.

❖ Empty the mixture into the prepared tin and bake for 45 minutes. Leave to cool in the tin and, when firm, cut into 16 squares.

PITHIVIERS (RUSTIC ALMOND TART)

100g (4oz, ⅔ cup) whole almonds,
blanched

100g (4oz) dried apricots

100g (4oz, ½ cup) sugar

75g (3oz, ⅓ cup) butter, at room
temperature

3 eggs

40g (1½ oz, ½ cup) cornflour

75g (3oz, ½ cup) apricot jam, sieved

25g (1oz, ⅓ cup) flaked almonds,
for decorating

☐ *Oven Temperature 180°C
(350°F, gas mark 4)*

✿ *Serves 6-8*

✗ *Not suitable for freezing*

❖ Preheat the oven and oil and line the base of a 20cm (8") diameter cake tin. Fit the Fine Grater Adaptor to the Mincer attachment on the Chef and grate the almonds and dried apricots into the Kenwood Bowl, alternating the two so that the almonds push the apricots through more easily.

❖ Add the sugar, butter, eggs and cornflour and beat for 2 minutes with the K Beater at speed 2.

❖ Pour into the prepared tin and bake for 25 minutes. Leave to cool in the tin for 10 minutes then turn out on to a wire rack.

❖ Warm the apricot jam and spread over the tart base. Decorate with the flaked almonds and serve immediately.

ALMOND & APRICOT ROULADE

❖ Preheat the oven then oil and line a 33cm x 23cm (13" x 9") Swiss Roll tin.

❖ Fit the Fine Grater Adaptor to the Mincer attachment on the Chef. Grate the almonds and reserve for later use.

❖ Separate the eggs, keeping the whites to one side. Put the egg yolks in the Kenwood Bowl, with 125g (4oz, ½ cup) of the sugar, then whisk using the Balloon Whisk at maximum speed until pale and fluffy. Stir in the vanilla essence and grated almonds.

❖ Sift the flour into the Bowl and lightly stir into the mixture. Pour the mixture out and leave to one side before thoroughly cleaning the Bowl. Pour in the egg whites and whisk at maximum speed until stiff but not dry. Gradually whisk in the remaining sugar.

❖ Use a large metal spoon to fold a quarter of the sugared egg white into the almond mixture. Then gently fold in the rest.

❖ Pour into the prepared tin and bake for 20 minutes until risen and golden. Cover with a layer of non-stick paper and a damp tea cloth, then leave in a cool place.

❖ When cool, remove the tea cloth and paper, leaving the sponge in the tin. Carefully roll up the sponge from one end to the other and hold for a few seconds, then unroll until it is flat again. This makes the sponge more flexible to roll when the filling has been added.

❖ Drizzle the Amaretto over the top of the sponge then pour on the yoghurt and spread over in a layer.

❖ Drain the apricots, if using a can, or halve and stone fresh ones. Cut the apricots into small pieces and scatter over the top of the yoghurt.

❖ With the help of the non-stick lining paper, roll up the roulade until it forms a log. Tip out onto a serving dish and sprinkle with a little caster sugar before serving.

100g (4oz, ⅔ cup) whole almonds blanched

5 eggs

150g (5oz, ⅔ cup) caster sugar

5ml (1 tsp) vanilla essence

45ml (3 tbsp) plain flour

45ml (3tbsp) Amaretto di Saronno, almond liqueur

275g (10oz, 1½ cups) Greek-style natural yoghurt

1 x 400g (14oz) can apricots, or 6 fresh ripe apricots

extra caster sugar, for decorating

☐ Oven Temperature 180°C (350°F, gas mark 4)

☺ Serves 4-6

✗ Not suitable for freezing

Suppenudeln

Soup in Germany is often served with the gratings from raw pasta dough. This recipe explains how to make the noodles - try adding them to a clear vegetable soup or consommé.

2 eggs
pinch of salt
175-225g (6-8oz, 1½-1¼ cups)
plain white flour

✿ *Serves 2*
✗ *Not suitable for freezing*

❖ Place the eggs and the salt in the Kenwood Bowl and use the K Beater at speed 1 to gradually mix in the flour. Add enough flour to make a firm, not wet, dough.

❖ Leave the dough to rest, wrapped in plastic film for 1 hour.

❖ Fit the Fine Grater Adaptor to the Mincer attachment on the Chef. Pull off small pieces of the dough and feed through the Mincer tube, collecting the grated dough in a dry cloth. Add to the soup 5 minutes before serving.

Potato Pancakes

900g (2 lb) potatoes, peeled
3 eggs
15ml (1 tbsp) plain flour
30ml (2 tbsp) soured cream
2.5ml (½ tsp) salt
oil, for frying
sugar, lemon or apple purée, for serving

○ *Makes 8 pancakes*
✗ *Not suitable for freezing*

❖ Fit the Fine Grater Adaptor to the Mincer attachment on the Chef placing a bowl and sieve underneath. Cut the potatoes into small chunks and grate them straight into the sieve so that the liquid drains into the bowl. Press down on the grated potato with the back of a spoon to remove any remaining liquid.

❖ Separate the eggs and keep the whites to one side. Stir the yolks into the grated potato with the plain flour, soured cream and salt. Whisk the egg whites at maximum speed until soft peaks form then gently fold into the potato mixture.

❖ Heat a little oil in a frying pan and place a heaped tablespoon of the potato mixture in the hot pan. Flatten into a thick pancake shape and fry until golden on each side. Serve hot with sugar and lemon, or apple purée.

SLICING GREEN BEANS & CITRUS PEEL

The Bean & Peel Slicer has two fundamental uses – one caters for green or runner bean enthusiasts, the other for marmalade makers.

Runner beans are long flat green beans which are mostly available in Britain, USA and France. They can grow to lengths of 25cm (10") or more and should be picked before they have ripened as the older they become the more string-like they get.

The secret of cooking runner beans is in how they are prepared. Long thin strips of roughly the same thickness is what is required and by hand this can be difficult. The Bean & Peel Slicer cuts green beans perfectly, ready for cooking either by boiling, steaming or stir-frying.

If you have ever made marmalade then you know what a laborious task it is to cut the peel into even shreds. The Bean & Peel Slicer will neatly cut your citrus peel, not just oranges but limes, grapefruits and lemons, into shreds of either a fine, medium or coarse thickness which can then be mixed into the preserve to add texture and flavour.

HINTS & TIPS

❖ Try the Bean & Peel Slicer for slicing peppers and other vegetables for Julienne strips which are ideal for decoration or stir-fries.

❖ Make sure you assemble the attachment correctly for use, with the relevant size of blade, corresponding 'comb' and plastic cog firmly in position, before securing the lid. The instruction leaflet supplied with the attachment contains full details for assembly and cleaning.

❖ Use the Bean & Peel Slicer between speeds 2 to 3.

LIME & LEMON MARMALADE

❖ Peel the limes and lemons, cutting the peel into strips small enough to pass through the Bean & Peel Slicer.

❖ Halve the fruit and extract the juice (the Citrus Juicer makes this a very easy job).

❖ Chop all that remains from the fruit halves and place in a small pan together with the pips and pulp left over from juicing the fruit. Add half the quantity of water and bring to the boil. Simmer gently for 1 hour, leaving the pan uncovered.

❖ Meanwhile, pass the peel through the Bean & Peel Slicer using the finest cutter blade. Place the strips in a very large heavy-based pan with the extracted juice and the remaining water.

❖ Bring to the boil and simmer gently, uncovered, for 1 hour or until the peel is soft. Remove from the heat, and add the sugar.

❖ Pour the liquid from the small pan through a metal sieve into the large pan, pressing down to extract as much of the thick, sticky liquid as possible. This stage is very important as the sticky substance is pectin, which is responsible for setting the marmalade. Be very thorough, pass some of the liquid through the sieve a second time if necessary, but do make sure the pith is left behind or else the marmalade will not be clear.

❖ Return the large pan to a gentle heat and stir until all the sugar has dissolved. At this point, turn the heat up to the highest setting and leave the pan to simmer furiously for 10 minutes. Watch carefully as the marmalade may overflow if the pan is not large enough.

❖ Remove the pan from the heat and test to see if the marmalade has set. To do this, give it a good stir and pour a little on to a cold plate. Leave this to cool for a short while, then test by touching it with your finger - the skin which has now formed will wrinkle if it is set. If not, boil for a further 5 minutes and repeat this process until a set is obtained.

❖ Leave the marmalade to cool for 30 minutes, then stir again and pour into clean, sterilised and warmed jars. Seal immediately and store in a cool dark place. Marmalade will last for several months like this.

6 limes

3 lemons

1.75 litres (3 pints, 6¼ cups) water

1.4kg (3lb, 6¼ cups) sugar

❍ *Makes approximately 4 x 450g (1lb) jars of marmalade*

✗ *Not suitable for freezing*

ORANGE MARMALADE

675g (1½ lb) oranges
2 lemons
1.4 litres (2½ pints, 5½ cups) water
1.1kg (2½ lb, 5½ cups) brown sugar

○ Makes approximately
4 x 450g (1lb) jars of marmalade
✗ Not suitable for freezing

❖ Proceed with the method for Lime & Lemon Marmalade, but using the medium-sized cutter blade in the Bean & Peel Slicer.

GREEN BEAN & CHERRY TOMATO STIR-FRY

250g (9oz) long, green runner
beans, topped and tailed
2 rashers bacon, rind removed
15ml (1 tbsp) vegetable oil
2 cloves garlic, crushed
10ml (2 tsp) sesame seeds
10ml (2 tsp) light soy sauce
100g (4oz) cherry tomatoes,
halved

✿ Serves 4
✗ Not suitable for freezing

❖ Wash and dry the beans. Pass them through the Bean & Peel Slicer using the coarse cutter blade and put to one side.

❖ Chop the bacon and prepare the rest of the ingredients, ready for use.

❖ Heat the oil in a wok and sauté the garlic until golden. Add the bacon and sesame seeds and stir-fry for 3 minutes until golden and crisp.

❖ Add the sliced beans and soy sauce and stir-fry for a further 5 minutes or until the beans are cooked.

❖ Stir in the tomatoes and heat through. Serve immediately with rice or noodles.

Breakfast Marmalade

CANS - EASY DINING, FUN RESULTS

Canned food can be a valuable part of any well-balanced and healthy diet. A cupboard well stocked with canned tuna, tomatoes, coconut milk, kidney beans and a variety of other pulses will always enable you to provide a meal with relative ease and without too much expense.

Often, canned foods can be a way of enticing children to eat the varieties of food which are essential to their growth and well being. One example is fish, which many children are not fond of in its fresh form because of the bones but a can of tuna and a spoonful of mayonnaise sandwiched together is a completely different story.

Pulses are a vital source of many proteins and are also rich in fibre. They need to be soaked well before cooking and this can easily be forgotten, until it is too late. Canned pulses make an excellent substitute and in addition, take less time to cook than freshly soaked pulses.

The Can Opener opens cans effortlessly leaving no jagged edges. The can is held in position until it is ready to be lifted away and the lid is retained by a magnet so that you don't have to dip your fingers in the can to remove it. As the attachment sits quite high above the work surface when mounted on the Chef, you can open larger and heavier cans as well as cans of different shapes.

HINTS & TIPS

❖ Always choose cans which are undamaged.

❖ Once a can has been opened, transfer the contents to a separate container for storage as the inside of the can may taint the flavour of the food once it is opened and no longer airtight.

❖ If you suffer from painful hands, due to arthritis or any other condition, this attachment is much easier to use than the conventional manual type.

❖ Leave the Can Opener permanently in position on the Chef so that it's always ready to use.

❖ Use the Can Opener at minimum speed.

Tuna Fish Casserole

A quick, healthy and delicious family supper - a real favourite in our household.

❖ Preheat the oven. Cook the macaroni until it is 'al dente'. Drain and place in a large bowl.

❖ Stir in the rest of the ingredients except the cracker biscuits, then tip the mixture into an ovenproof baking dish. Sprinkle with the broken cracker biscuits if desired, and bake for 25-30 minutes until hot and bubbling.

450g (1lb) macaroni

2 x 295g (11oz) can condensed cream of mushroom soup

1 x 400g (14oz) can tuna chunks in brine or oil, drained

2 tomatoes, roughly chopped

10ml (2 tsp) Worcestershire sauce

4 cracker biscuits, broken into small pieces, optional

☐ Oven Temperature 180°C (350°F, gas mark 4)

✪ Serves 4-6

✗ Not suitable for freezing

Thai Vegetable Curry

❖ Heat the coconut milk in a pan with the stock cube, lime leaves and lemon grass.

❖ When simmering, add the potato and cook for 5 minutes.

❖ Stir in the sliced leek and simmer for a further 5 minutes.

❖ Add the mangetout and simmer for a final 2 minutes. Stir in the cashew nuts and chopped coriander, then serve with rice.

1 x 400g (14oz) can coconut milk

1 Tom Yam stock cube, available at Thai food stores

2 lime leaves, optional

1 stalk lemon grass, bruised, optional

100g (4oz) potato, peeled and cut into 5mm (⅕") cubes

1 leek, sliced into 1cm (½") pieces

100g (4oz) mangetout, topped and tailed

50g (2oz, ¼ cup) cashew nuts

30ml (2 tbsp) fresh coriander, chopped

✪ Serves 2 as a main course or 4 as an accompaniment

✗ Not suitable for freezing

SPICY BEEF HOT POT

This is an all-in-one pot meal which is thick and tasty but also healthy.

325g (12oz) stewing beef, cut into 3cm (1¼") cubes

2 x 400g (14oz) cans Mulligatawny, beef curry soup

25g (1oz, ¼ cup) pearl barley

1 medium onion, peeled and thinly sliced

4 carrots, peeled and sliced

salt and freshly milled black pepper

☐ *Oven Temperature 150°C (300°F, gas mark 2)*

✪ *Serves 4*

✻ *Suitable for freezing*

❖ Preheat the oven. Place all the ingredients in a casserole pot, stir well, cover, and bake for 2 hours. Serve with potatoes, rice, or pasta.

INDIVIDUAL SHERRY TRIFLES

6 trifle sponges

1 x 400g (14oz) can raspberries, in syrup

45ml (3 tbsp) sherry

1 large banana, sliced

1 x 400g (14oz) can custard

90ml (6 tbsp) double cream, lightly whipped

◯ *Makes 6 trifles*

✗ *Not suitable for freezing*

❖ Break up the trifle sponges and place in the base of 6 ramekin dishes or dessert glasses.

❖ Drain the raspberries and reserve the syrup. Spoon 30ml (2 tbsp) of the raspberry syrup and 7.5ml (½ tbsp) of the sherry over the sponges in each of the dishes or glasses.

❖ Divide the banana and the drained raspberries equally between the 6 dishes. Spoon the custard over the banana, making sure it is well covered.

❖ Cover with plastic film and chill for 12 hours or overnight in a refrigerator.

❖ Just before serving, top with the whipped cream.

SCREAMS FOR ICE CREAM

"My tongue is smiling" - Abigail Trillin aged four, after eating chocolate ice-cream

It was the Chinese who first taught the Arabic people the art of making iced drinks and desserts. They would use snow and ice conserved from the winter months in specially built ice caves to produce iced delicacies to last throughout the long hot summer. It was not, however, until the 13th century that Marco Polo brought to Europe, the secret of cooling, using water and saltpeter. Thus in Italy, the great fashion of water ices began.

To make ice cream and water ices with velvety smoothness the mixture must be kept moving while it freezes, which prevents the formation of ice crystals. The Ice Cream Maker, with its rotating paddle, is able to do just that, turning the mixture into a lovely soft ice in a very short time.

There are four main bases used to make ice cream: rich traditional custard, water syrup (for sorbets), flavoursome cream and yoghurt.

Many custard ice creams call for a standard custard base which can be made using the recipe below.

HINTS & TIPS

❖ Once ice cream is made it can be kept in a plastic container in the freezer. To soften, transfer the ice cream to a refrigerator for 30 minutes before serving.

❖ Always freeze the Ice Cream Maker bowl for at least 18-24 hours before use. Better still, keep it stored in the freezer at all times.

❖ Most ice cream takes between 15 and 30 minutes to make in the attachment. It can be eaten straight away as a 'soft scoop' or, if preferred, freeze for 20 minutes before serving.

NB. The Ice Cream Maker Attachment can only be used with round, Kenlyte bowls.

BASIC CUSTARD FOR ICE CREAM

300ml (½ pint, 1¼ cups) milk
15ml (1 tbsp) sugar
few drops of vanilla essence
2 egg yolks

❖ Heat the milk, sugar and vanilla in a pan until hot, but not boiling.

❖ Meanwhile, place the egg yolks in a bowl. When the milk mixture is ready, pour it over the egg yolks, stirring continuously until the mixture is smooth.

❖ Return the mixture to the pan over a low heat. Stir constantly until the mixture thickens enough to coat the back of a wooden spoon. The custard is now ready to be used.

CREAM OF COCONUT ICE CREAM

Part of my Masterchef winning menu, it took months to develop the coconut flavour of this ice cream. It turns out really thick and creamy because of the white chocolate - funny how some things take so long!

❖ Place the white chocolate pieces, coconut milk powder, egg yolks and milk in a pan and heat gently. Stir continuously, making sure it does not simmer, until thick and smooth.

❖ Stir in the double cream and liqueur, if desired, then chill in the refrigerator.

❖ Place the Ice Cream Maker in position on the Chef and switch to minimum speed. Pour the mixture through the feed tube and churn until it resembles freshly whipped cream.

❖ Serve immediately or keep in a plastic container in the freezer, then place in the refrigerator for 30 minutes before serving.

100g (4oz) white chocolate, broken into pieces
75g (3oz, ¾ cup) coconut milk powder
2 egg yolks
300ml (½ pint, 1¼ cups) milk
300ml (½ pint, 1¼ cups) double cream
15ml (1 tbsp) Malibu, coconut rum, optional

✿ *Serves 4-6*
❈ *Suitable for freezing*

CHOCOLATE CARAMEL BAR ICE CREAM

❖ Slice the chocolate bars and place in a large pan with the milk, then heat, stirring constantly until the chocolate bar slices have melted and the mixture is smooth.

❖ Stir in the double cream, leave to cool then chill in the refrigerator until cold.

❖ Place the Ice Cream Maker in position on the Chef and switch to minimum speed. Pour the mixture through the feed tube and churn until it resembles freshly whipped cream.

❖ Serve immediately or keep in a plastic container in the freezer, then place in the refrigerator for 30 minutes before serving.

2 chocolate, nutty caramel bars, such as Snickers, total weight 130g (4½oz)
150ml (¼ pint, ½ cup) milk
150ml (¼ pint, ½ cup) double cream

✿ *Serves 2-4*
❈ *Suitable for freezing*

INDIAN PISTACHIO NUT ICE CREAM

300ml (½ pint, 1¼ cups) double cream

300ml (½ pint, 1¼ cups) milk

1 x 400g (14oz) can sweetened condensed milk

15ml (1 tbsp) clear honey

30ml (2 tbsp) pistachio nuts, chopped

10ml (2 tsp) rose water

✿ *Serves 4-6*
✳ *Suitable for freezing*

❖ Heat the double cream, milk, condensed milk and honey together in a large heavy-based pan. Bring to a simmer, stirring constantly to prevent burning. Simmer gently for 45 minutes, stirring occasionally.

❖ Remove from the heat and stir in the pistachio nuts and rose water. Cool in a refrigerator for at least 2 hours or until completely cold. This mixture can even be left to cool overnight.

❖ Place the Ice Cream Maker in position on the Chef and switch to minimum speed. Pour the mixture through the feed tube and churn until it resembles freshly whipped cream.

❖ Serve immediately or keep in a plastic container in the freezer, then place in the refrigerator for 30 minutes before serving.

VANILLA CREOLE ICE CREAM

A rich vanilla ice cream with a tangy flavour of crème fraîche.

200g (7oz, ¾ cup) crème fraîche

575ml (1 pint, 2¼ cups) custard, canned or freshly made

few drops of vanilla essence

75g (3oz, ⅓ cup) caster sugar

✿ *Serves 8-10*
✳ *Suitable for freezing*

❖ Mix together all the ingredients in a large jug. If you wish to make your own custard, use the method given on page 144 in place of canned custard. Chill the mixture in the refrigerator until cold.

❖ Place the Ice Cream Maker in position on the Chef and switch to minimum speed. Pour the mixture through the feed tube and churn until it resembles freshly whipped cream.

❖ Serve immediately or keep in a plastic container in the freezer, then place in the refrigerator for 30 minutes before serving.

CHOCOLATE CREOLE ICE CREAM

❖ Add 225g (8oz) melted milk chocolate to the above recipe, omitting the sugar.

FUDGE CREOLE ICE CREAM

❖ Melt 450g (1lb) fudge with 45ml (3 tbsp) milk over a low heat and add to the above recipe, omitting the sugar.

MISSISSIPPI MUD PIE

❖ Preheat the oven to the first temperature. Make the pastry by putting the flour and butter in the Kenwood Bowl and mixing, with the K Beater at speed 1, until the mixture resembles bread-crumbs.

❖ Add the 25g (1oz, ⅛ cup) sugar, and the cocoa powder and mix again, pouring in enough water to make a pastry. Roll out the dough on a floured surface, to form a circle large enough to line a 23cm (9") flan tin.

❖ Press the pastry into the flan tin, then bake blind for 25 minutes until crisp and golden. Remove from the oven and leave to cool completely.

❖ Meanwhile, take the ice creams from the freezer and place in the refrigerator for 30 minutes to soften. Pile scoops of ice cream, using alternate flavours, into the cooled pastry case, pressing into a rounded dome shape.

❖ Return the ice cream pie to the freezer until you have prepared the meringue. If you are preparing it in advance you may leave it in the freezer at this stage, but do cover it well.

❖ Turn the oven to its second temperature and use the Balloon Whisk at maximum speed to beat the egg whites until they form soft peaks. Add the 175g (6oz, ¾ cup) sugar while the Whisk is still turning and continue whisking until the meringue is stiff.

❖ Take the pie from the freezer and spoon the meringue over the top, making sure that it covers the whole surface of the ice cream. Bake for 5 minutes, by which time the meringue should have turned golden. Serve immediately.

PASTRY BASE:

175g (6oz, 1⅓ cups) plain flour
75g (3oz, ⅓ cup) butter
25g (1oz, ⅛ cup) caster sugar
15ml (1 tbsp) cocoa powder
water

TOPPING:

½ quantity of Vanilla Creole Ice Cream
½ quantity of Chocolate Creole Ice Cream
½ quantity of Fudge Creole Ice Cream

MERINGUE:

3 egg whites
175g (6oz, ¾ cup) caster sugar

☐ *Oven Temperature*
  firstly 200°C (400°F, gas mark 6)
  then 230°C (450°F, gas mark 8)

✪ *Serves 6-8*

❄ *Suitable for freezing*

APPLE, CINNAMON & YOGHURT ICE

325g (12oz) cooking apples,
peeled, cored and sliced
2.5ml (½ tsp) cinnamon powder
3 strips of lemon zest
150ml (¼ pint, ½ cup) cider,
white wine or apple juice
50g (2oz, ⅓ cup) demerara
sugar
60ml (4 tbsp) clear honey
90ml (6 tbsp) Greek-style
natural yoghurt

✿ *Serves 4-6*
✳ *Suitable for freezing*

❖ Place the apple slices in a pan and add the cinnamon, lemon zest and the cider, white wine or apple juice. Cover and simmer gently for 10 minutes or until the apples turn to pulp.

❖ Remove from heat, take out the lemon zest and stir in the sugar, honey and yoghurt.

❖ Chill the mixture until it is completely cold.

❖ Place the Ice Cream Maker in position on the Chef and switch to minimum speed. Pour the mixture through the feed tube and churn until it resembles freshly whipped cream.

❖ Serve immediately or keep in a plastic container in the freezer, then place in the refrigerator for 30 minutes before serving.

MANGO & LIME SORBET

2 ripe mangos
60ml (4 tbsp) lime juice
50g (2oz, ½ cup) icing sugar

✿ *Serves 4*
✳ *Suitable for freezing*

❖ Peel the mangos and remove the flesh from the stone. Blend the mango with the lime juice and sugar in the Liquidiser until smooth.

❖ Place the Ice Cream Maker in position on the Chef and switch to minimum speed. Pour the mixture through the feed tube and churn until thickened.

❖ Serve immediately or keep in a plastic container in the freezer, then place in the refrigerator for 30 minutes before serving.

BANANA, ORANGE & LEMON SORBET

1 banana, peeled
juice of 1 orange
juice of 1 lemon
50g (2oz, ¼ cup) sugar

✿ *Serves 4*
✳ *Suitable for freezing*

❖ Place all the ingredients together in the Liquidiser and blend until smooth.

❖ Place the Ice Cream Maker in position on the Chef and switch to minimum speed. Pour the mixture through the feed tube and churn until thickened.

❖ Serve immediately or keep in a plastic container in the freezer, then place in the refrigerator for 30 minutes before serving.

Cream of Coconut
Ice Cream

Conversion Charts

Weight

Metric	Imperial	Metric	Imperial
10g	½ oz	275g	10oz
20g	¾ oz	300g	11oz
25g	1oz	325g	12oz
40g	1½ oz	375g	13oz
50g	2oz	400g	14oz
70g	2½ oz	425g	15oz
75g	3oz	450g	1lb
100g	4oz	550g	1¼lb
150g	5oz	675g	1½lb
175g	6oz	775g	1¾lb
200g	7oz	900g	2lb
225g	8oz	1kg	2¼lb
250g	9oz		

Volume

Metric	Imperial	Metric	Imperial
15ml	½ fl oz	350ml	12fl oz
30ml	1fl oz	375ml	13fl oz
45ml	1½ fl oz	400ml	14fl oz
60ml	2fl oz	425ml	¾ pint
85ml	3fl oz	475ml	16fl oz
115ml	4fl oz	500ml	17fl oz
150ml	¼ pint	525ml	18fl oz
175ml	6fl oz	550ml	19fl oz
200ml	7fl oz	575ml	1 pint
225ml	8fl oz	725ml	1¼ pints
250ml	9fl oz	825ml	1½ pints
300ml	½ pint	1 litre	1¾ pints
325ml	11fl oz		

g = gram(s) **oz** = ounce(s)

kg = kilogram(s) **lb** = pound(s)

ml = millilitre(s) **fl oz** = fluid ounce(s)

Conversion Charts

American Cups

Item	Cups	Metric	Imperial
liquid, milk, water etc.	⅛	30 ml	1 fl oz
	¼	60 ml	2 fl oz
	⅓	80 ml	3 fl oz
	½	115 ml	4 fl oz
	1	250 ml	9 fl oz
flour & icing sugar	¼	25 g	1 oz
	½	50 g	2 oz
	1	100 g	4 oz
sugar – white granulated & caster	¼	50 g	2 oz
	½	100 g	4 oz
	1	225 g	8 oz
sugar – brown & demerera	¼	40 g	1½ oz
	½	75 g	3 oz
	1	175 g	6 oz
breadcrumbs	¼	10 g	½ oz
	½	25 g	1 oz
	1	50 g	2 oz
butter	¼	50 g	2 oz
	½	100 g	4 oz
	1	225 g	8 oz
other ingredients	calculated individually using genuine American cups		

Measurements

Metric	Imperial
1 cm	½"
2.5 cm	1"
5 cm	2"
10 cm	4"
20 cm	8"
25 cm	10"

cm = centimetre(s)
" = inch(es)

Spoon Measures

Metric	Imperial
1.25 ml	¼ tsp
2.5 ml	½ tsp
2.75 ml	¾ tsp
5 ml	1 tsp
10 ml	2 tsp
15 ml	1 tbsp
30 ml	2 tbsp

tsp = teaspoon(s)
tbsp = tablespoon(s)

Oven Temperatures

°C	°F	Gas Mark
140	275	1
150	300	2
170	325	3
180	350	4
190	375	5
200	400	6
220	425	7
230	450	8
240	475	9

For cooking ranges, run by solid fuel, gas or oil, please consult your range burner manual.

Key to Symbols

□ = oven temperatures in °C, °F, and gas mark.

✪ = number of servings, i.e. number of people it will serve.

◯ = amount or number of items made, eg. 9" cake or 15 biscuits

✳ = finished recipe is suitable for freezing

✗ = finished recipe is not suitable for freezing

❖ = Gluten free (Grain Mill only)

✿ = Not Gluten free (Grain Mill only)

All attachments and accessories for the Chef, including the Bowl and Spatula are distinguished from other utensils by the use of capital letters.

All measurements in this book have been individually calculated and rounded to the nearest workable quantity as shown in these charts. When following a recipe always use one set of measurements. Do not mix metric with imperial.

GLOSSARY

Whilst every effort has been made to include only internationally known ingredients in this book, some items may be more difficult to find in certain countries. This glossary has been compiled to help with the understanding of less common ingredients and cooking terms, and the suggestion of alternative ingredients for use in various recipes.

'al Dente' – an Italian expression which describes the degree to which pasta should be cooked, ie. until it is still firm to the bite

Amaretto di Saronno – an Italian Liqueur flavoured with almonds, apricots and aromatic extracts

Anchovy Essence – can be substituted with anchovy purée which can be made by blending water with canned anchovies to make a smooth paste

Aubergine – otherwise known as Egg Plant or Brinjal

Bacon – otherwise known as Cured Pork, generally available in slices (rashers)

Bain Marie – a pan of hot, not boiling, water used to heat a second pan for the gentle cooking or warming of sauces, soups or mixtures

Baking Blind (Blind-Baking) – cooking an empty pastry flan case before it is filled – after lining the tin with pastry, either chill well and bake in a hot oven, or line with baking parchment and fill with baking beans to help the pastry keep its shape during baking

Baking Dish – usually oblong in shape, with deep sides, for retaining the sauce

Baking Powder – a raising agent consisting of bicarbonate of soda (baking soda) mixed with cream of tartar (tartaric acid)

Baking Sheet – a tray with slightly raised edges for cooking biscuits, cakes etc. Unless they are non-stick coated, baking sheets need to be oiled or lined with baking parchment to prevent sticking

Baking Soda – otherwise known as Bicarbonate of Soda

Barbecue – traditionally a charcoal burner used outdoors for grilling (broiling) meat, fish or vegetables to give a charred or blackened outer skin

Batch – the correct quantity of ingredients which can be comfortably mixed or processed in a bowl or attachment

Beef Stock – otherwise known as Bouillon (see 'Stock')

Bicarbonate of Soda (Baking Soda) a main ingredient in baking powder, sometimes used on its own

Blanched Almonds – almonds with their skins removed

Blanching – lightly cooking vegetables or nuts in boiling water either to help remove skin or to serve as a first stage of cooking, in the preparation of many dishes

Blue Cheese – a soft blue-veined cheese, mostly made from cow's milk, eg Stilton, Roquefort

Brandy (**Cognac, Armagnac**)	–	a spirit distilled from wine
Breadcrumbs	–	small particles of bread used for stuffings and other dishes
Brie Cheese	–	a French full-fat cheese made from cow's milk, which has a soft texture inside and a soft white crust
Brine	–	a solution of water and salt (and sometimes sugar or flavourings) for preserving meat, fish or vegetables
Bruising	–	crushing the end of a stalk such as lemon grass or garlic to release the flavours
Buckwheat (**Saracen Corn, Blé Noir, Beaucuit or Bucail**)	–	a dark cereal resembling beech nuts
Bulgur Wheat (**Burghul, Cracked Wheat**)	–	a wholewheat grain incorporating the wheatgerm which has been cooked, dried and cracked
Cajun Spices	–	a ready-made mixture of spices from the Southern states of America, main ingredients being chilli powder, dried pimentos, pepper, garlic powder, ginger and allspice - can be substituted with any Mexican, Creole or Jamaican spice mix
Capers	–	a flower bud which is either pickled in vinegar or preserved in brine, and used as a condiment in many dishes
Caramelised	–	sugar when it has been gently heated until it turns to caramel, or vegetables when cooked in sugar and water, or butter, until glazed
Caraway Seed (**Meadow Cumin, Fool's Aniseed**)	–	an aromatic seed used to flavour breads, cakes and liqueurs
Caster Sugar (**Fine or Superfine Sugar**)	–	refined white sugar which is finer than granulated but coarser than icing sugar
Cayenne Pepper	–	a variety of pepper with a strong, hot flavour mostly available in ground form - can be substituted with mild chilli powder
Celeriac (**Celery Root or Céleri-rave**)	–	a variety of celery with a characteristic white flesh which is often grated
Celery	–	a vegetable cultivated for its white fibrous stalk, although the leaves, roots and seeds are also used in cooking
Charred	–	cooked until blackened in colour
Cheddar Cheese	–	a full-fat, medium hard cheese, from England but produced worldwide - can be substituted with Gruyère, Emmental or Vegetarian Cheddar

Cherry Tomato	–	a small, full-flavoured cocktail tomato
Chicken Stock	–	otherwise known as Bouillon (see 'Stock')
Chinese Five Spice Powder	–	a ready-made mixture of sweet aromatic spices available in oriental food stores, main ingredients being star anise, fennel, cinnamon, cloves, sechuan and peppercorns
Chinese Stem Ginger	–	ginger root preserved in syrup
Chive	–	a green herb related to the spring onion family, whose leaves are chopped and used as seasoning
Cider	–	a sparkling alcoholic drink produced from the fermentation of apples – can be substituted in many dishes with still or sparkling apple juice
Coarse	–	term used to describe a larger cut, when shredding, slicing, chopping etc.
Coconut Milk Powder	–	a dried powder made from coconut milk, used to flavour a variety of dishes – can be substituted with creamed coconut
Condensed Soup	–	a soup concentrate usually double the strength
Coriander (Cilantro)	–	a leafy green aromatic herb
Coriander Seeds	–	an aromatic seed produced from the coriander plant
Courgette (Zucchini)	–	a variety of marrow usually eaten when young
Cornmeal	–	a cereal used to make 'polenta'
Creaming Together	–	the method of combining butter and sugar to obtain a light airy mixture
Crème de Menthe	–	a mint-flavoured liqueur
Crème Fraîche	–	a French variety of cream made from cow's milk, with a thick consistency and sharp flavour – can be substituted with soured cream
Croûton	–	small piece of bread which has been toasted and lightly fried or baked – used in salads and soups
Crumb	–	consistency of a dry ingredient after milling or blending
Curd Cheese	–	a soft and smooth, full-fat cheese with a slightly sharp flavour – can be substituted with cream cheese mixed with a few drops of lemon juice
Custard (Crème Anglaise)	–	a thick, sweet sauce used in desserts – traditionally made with eggs, milk and sugar and sometimes cream and flour, though instant custard powder (flavoured cornflour) is now commonly used as a quick alternative
Demerera Sugar	–	a soft light brown sugar
Deseeded	–	fruit or vegetables with the pips, seeds or stones removed
Desiccated Coconut	–	coconut which has been dried and shredded

Dessert Apple	–	a sweet eating apple such as Cox's, Braeburn, Golden Delicious, Granny Smith
Dicing	–	chopping ingredients into small, even-sized pieces or cubes
Digestive Biscuits	–	sweetmeal biscuits with a nutty flavour, traditionally made with soda to aid digestion
Double Cream (Heavy Cream)	–	a full-fat (48%) thick cream, most widely used for its versatility – it can be heated, whipped, soured or used to make butter
Dusting	–	using a sieve or strainer to sprinkle icing sugar over a finished cake or dish for decoration, or to sprinkle flour into an oiled baking tin to help prevent sticking
Emmental Cheese	–	a full-fat, medium hard cheese originating from Switzerland
Evaporated Milk	–	a concentrated, homogenised milk with a distinctive flavour, which is versatile due to its long shelf life
Feta Cheese	–	a full-fat white cheese traditionally made from the milk of ewes or goats, originating from Greece
Filo Pastry	–	a delicate pastry made from flour, water, egg and a little oil, formed into a dough and rolled out until it is paper thin – often bought frozen in sheets
Fine	–	term used to describe a smaller cut when shredding, slicing, chopping etc.
Flageolet Beans	–	a variety of bean, available dried or canned – can be substituted with haricot beans
Flaked Almonds	–	thinly sliced almonds
Flan Tin		usually circular, with shallow sides for baking pies, pastries and flans
Folding In	–	gently mixing in an ingredient such as flour to creamed butter and sugar in order to retain the air which has been beaten into the mixture
Fructose	–	a natural fruit sugar
Fudge	–	a soft, non-sticky caramel made from sugar, butter and condensed milk
Garam Masala	–	a ready-made mixture of aromatic oriental spices
Gelatine	–	available in the form of powder or a dried sheet and used as a thickener or stabiliser – can be substituted with agar agar as a vegetarian alternative – follow the instructions on the packet for reconstitution
Glacé Cherries	–	cherries preserved in syrup
Glazing	–	applying a substance to food to create a glossy appearance, eg. cooking vegetables in either sugar and water or butter, or brushing egg on pastry or cakes before cooking
Gluten	–	part of the wheat which is viscous or sticky – gluten free recipes contain no gluten and are suitable for those who may have an allergic reaction to gluten
Glycerine	–	a thick, clear liquid with a slightly sweet flavour – mostly used for medicinal purposes but also used in cookery to preserve the soft texture of substances such as Royal or Snow Icing – available at most pharmacies

Grating	–	reducing to fine or coarse threads, eg. cheese and carrots or to powder and small particles, eg. coconut and zest of lemon or orange
Gravy	–	term used for either a sauce made from meat juices or a thick or clear brown stock used in savoury dishes
Greasing	–	see 'Oiling'
Greek-Style Yoghurt (Yogurt, Yaourt)	–	a thick natural yoghurt used on its own or in cooking - popular due to its mild, creamy flavour
Green Pepper	–	a large, sweet, fleshy capsicum with a mild flavour - not to be confused with the small hot chilli pepper
Grilling (broiling)	–	a method of cooking using radiant heat directed either from above or below
Grinding	–	crushing ingredients to form small particles
Gruyère Cheese	–	a full-fat hard cheese originating from France and Switzerland
Jam	–	a preserve made with boiled fruit and sugar
Juice Concentrate	–	concentrated and usually sweetened fruit juice - diluted before drinking
Kirsch	–	a German white brandy distilled from cherries
Kneading	–	a gentle but firm mixing of a dough to make it softer and smoother and, to evenly distribute the raising agentt
Lasagne	–	a flat pasta formed into strips
Lemon grass	–	an oriental seasoning, often used whole with its stalk and bulb
Lime Leaves	–	leaves from the lime tree - can be substituted with lime zest
Lining a Tin	–	placing a layer of parchment in a tin to prevent the cake or bread, etc, from sticking during cooking - also, the term used for laying flattened pastry into a tin to form a base for pies, tarts or flans
Loaf Tin	–	rectangular high-sided tin for baking bread, loaves or cakes
Macaroni	–	small tubes of pasta - can be various sizes
Malibu	–	a white rum flavoured with coconut - can be substituted with coconut liqueur
Mangetout (Snow Peas, Sugar Peas)	–	flat green beans used whole in salads and stir-fries
Marinade	–	a sauce used for marinating - a process in which meat or other foods are soaked for a long or short period of time, prior to cooking, to tenderise or flavour
Marmalade	–	a preserve or jam made with citrus fruits
Milling	–	grinding a hard substance to form powder or small particles, eg. spices or flour
Millet	–	a variety of cereal grain rich in vitamins
Mince Pie Tin	–	flat tin with a number of indentations - used for baking individual pies or tarts

Mulligatawny	-	a spicy soup originating from India and traditionally made with chicken stock - now more widely known as beef curry soup
Oiling	-	brushing a tin or baking sheet with vegetable oil, butter or margarine to prevent sticking during cooking
Orange Flower Water	-	an aromatic liquid made from the fragrant flowers of the Seville orange - used as flavouring in cakes and biscuits
Ouzo	-	a Greek spirit flavoured with aniseed - can be substituted with Pastis, Pernod or Raki
Paprika	-	a spicy powdered seasoning made from a variety of mild sweet red pepper
Parchment	-	opaque paper used either for lining tins to prevent sticking, or wrapping cakes to prevent burning
Parmesan Cheese	-	an Italian medium-fat, hard cheese with a strong characteristic flavour
Pâté Dish	-	rectangular earthenware or china dish used for making pâté or terrine
Paw Paw	-	an exotic fruit similar to papaya, which can be used as a substitute
Pearl Barley	-	a cereal which has been hulled and milled until the grain resembles small pearls
Peel	-	the complete outer covering of a fruit or vegetable
Pestle and Mortar	-	traditional utensil used for crushing ingredients such as spices or nuts
Pith	-	the innermost white part of the peel of a citrus fruit
Plastic Film	-	flexible plasticised sheet used for covering food during storage or resting
Plum Tomato (Roma Tomato)	-	oval-shaped tomato with a strong flavour which is suitable for many dishes
Prawn (Shrimp)	-	a small grey shellfish, approximately 3cm (½") in size - turns pink when cooked
Prosciutto	-	an Italian cured, dried ham
Puffed Up	-	term used for bread dough which has been left to rise with the action of the yeast
Pulping	-	pulverising a substance by mashing, blending or crushing
Purée	-	a blended, strained or pressed ingredient with a smooth consistency
Puy Lentil	-	France's most popular lentil - can be substituted with any green or brown lentil
Rack of Lamb	-	7 ribs of lamb, often with one rib removed, for 2 equal servings
Ramekin	-	small round, straight-sided dish or pot made of earthenware, china or glass - used for individual dishes such as soufflé
Raspberry (Framboise)	-	cultivated in France, Britain and America - can be substituted with any other soft red berry

Red Pepper	-	a large, sweet, fleshy capsicum with a mild flavour - not to be confused with the small hot chilli pepper
Reducing	-	making a sauce or liquid more concentrated in flavour by evaporating some of the water, or making it thick and condensed in volume
Runner Beans	-	long green beans picked when young before the pods have developed - usually sliced then steamed, boiled or stir-fried
Rye	-	a cereal grain often mixed with wheat - used especially in Scandinavia and Russia for making crispbreads or dark textured bread
Sage	-	a green herb cultivated for its aromatic, slightly bitter-tasting leaves - used for flavouring meats, cheeses and drinks
Sausage Casing	-	see page 66
Sautéeing	-	frying ingredients in a frying pan or heavy-based saucepan until they turn brown
Screen	-	term used for part of an extruding or pressing attachment such as the Pasta Extruder or Colander & Sieve, giving a choice of shape or size of extrusion
Seasoning	-	adding condiments, such as salt and pepper, to a dish to enhance the flavour
Seeded	-	fruit or vegetables which still contain their seeds, pips or stones
Self Raising Flour	-	flour to which a raising agent has been added in order to facilitate the rising of cakes - can be substituted with plain flour and baking powder
Separating an Egg	-	cracking open an egg, and straining the white from the yolk
Sieve	-	a utensil made of silk, nylon or metal used for sifting flour or straining, sieving and puréeing fruit or cooked vegetables
Simmering	-	cooking food slowly and steadily over a gentle heat and keeping just below boiling point
Single Cream (Light Cream)	-	a low fat (18%) runny, pouring cream - used in coffee, soups or as a topping for desserts
Skewer	-	a long thin stick made of wood or metal - used for spearing food for cooking, eg. kebabs or for testing bread or cakes during baking
Soft Peaks	-	See page 38
Soured Cream (Smetana or Dairy Sour)	-	a low fat (18%) single cream, soured to give a tart, refreshing flavour - used in cooking or as a topping - can be substituted with French Crème Fraîche or German Sauere Sahne which has a slightly milder taste
Soya Bean	-	a pulse originating from the Far East now used increasingly more as a source of vegetable protein in vegetarian diets - a number of products are made from it such as milk, flour and cheese
Spelt Grain	-	see page 112

Squid Ink	–	a black substance obtained from squid (otherwise known as Calamar or Calamari) and used as a natural colourant for sauces and pasta
Stir-frying	–	frying ingredients quickly, at high temperature, and with little oil – a healthy way of cooking
Stock (Bouillon)	–	a flavoured liquid base made from either meat, poultry, fish or vegetables – used for making sauces, stews and other savoury dishes
Stock Cubes	–	solid extracts which can be dissolved in boiling water to give stock – designed to save time in cooking
Stoneground Wholemeal Bread Flour	–	a strong flour made from the whole wheat containing high levels of fibre and gluten – used especially for making bread
Strong White Bread Flour	–	a flour with high protein content and good gluten strength – its high water retention capacity makes it highly suitable for bread-making
Swede (Rotabaga, Rottabagge)	–	a root vegetable with orange-yellow flesh and a slightly sweet flavour – used in stews and savoury dishes or mashed and served as a side vegetable
Tagliatelle	–	flat, ribboned pasta
Tam Yam Stock Cube	–	a strong-flavoured enhancer, sold internationally under the Knorr brand of foods, which conjurs up the very essence of Thai cooking – can possibly be substituted with other Thai flavourings, but a better alternative is hard to find
Topping and Tailing	–	removing stalks and ends of vegetables or fruit such as gooseberries
Trifle Sponge	–	a light airy cake which is soaked in spirit and topped with fruit, custard and cream to make the popular dessert 'Trifle' – often available ready-made but can be substituted with a simple home-made recipe.
Tureen	–	deep, covered heatproof dish – used for serving soup
Turmeric (Curcuma, Curcumine)	–	a tropical aromatic plant whose powdered stem is used as a spice and a yellow colourant
Turnip	–	a fleshy yellow or white root vegetable with a distinctive flavour – used mainly in stews and casseroles
Vegetable Stock	–	see 'Stock'
Vegetarian Cheese	–	a cheese similar to Cheddar but made with non-animal derived enzymes, allowing its use in vegetarian diets
White Fish	–	where stipulated in a recipe any local white fish can be used such as halibut, huss, cod, hake, kingclip, whiting, coley, plaice or sole
Worcestershire Sauce	–	an English condiment, similar to Soy Sauce, made from malt vinegar, molasses, sugar, shallot, garlic, tamarind, clove, anchovy essence and meat extract – used as a seasoning in all types of dishes as well as in cocktails and drinks
Yeast Extract	–	a concentrated substance extracted from yeast
Zest	–	the outermost coloured part of the peel of a citrus fruit

FIRST COURSES

Avocado Mousse Pâté,	53
Cajun Style Hot Crab Soufflé	39
Chicken & Leek Stuffed Pancakes	42
Chicken Liver Pâté with Green Olives	53
Coarse Country Pâté	63
Crispy Duck Parcels with Orange Sauce	62
Potted Gruyère	76
Soured Cream Blue Cheese and Chive Dip	121
Stuffed Mussels	91

SOUPS

Bortsch	50
Carrot & Lemon Soup	77
Celeriac & Blue Cheese Soup	49
Cream of Courgette and Spinach Soup	121
Fisherman's Shrimp Bisque	49
Gazpacho	51
Instant Spring Vegetable Soup	50
Suppenudeln	134
Winter Vegetable Soup	102

BREADS

Bagels	35
Barley Malt Loaf	113
Frying Pan Naan Bread	34
Irish Soda Bread	28
Mediterranean Fruit Bread	36
Mixed Wholegrain Loaf	31
Potato Focaccia Bread	27
Prosciutto & Parmesan Bread	33
Rye Bread	31
Spelt Flour Bread	112
Sweet Irish Soda Bread	28
Zopf (Swiss Sunday Bread)	32

PASTA DISHES

Herb Pasta	95
Macaroni with Raisins & Apricot	98
Oriental Chicken & Cashew Nut Salad	97
Pasta al Nero di Seppia	95
Pasta Rossa	95
Pasta Verde	95
Plain Pasta	95
Tagliatelle with Chicken Liver, Capers & Sage	98
Three Tomato & Feta Rigatoni	97
Vegetarian Lentil Lasagne	96
Wholemeal Pasta	95

MAIN COURSES:

MEAT

American Meatloaf (with Onion Gravy)	61
Beef & Black Pepper Sausages	70
Herb Butter Beefburgers	59
Kashmiri Koftas in Flaked Almonds with Spicy Yoghurt Sauce	60
Lamb, Rosemary & Lemon Sausages	67
Lamb topped with a Herb Crust	54
Meat Kebbe	72
Pork, Fennel & Paprika Sausages	67
Sausage & Potato Casserole	107
Spicy Beef Hot Pot	142

POULTRY

Cajun Style Chicken Meatballs	63
Chicken, Lemon & Chive Sausages	70
Chicken & Leek Stuffed Pancakes	42
Chicken Tikka Kebabs	90
Chinese Chicken Sausages	68
Curried Chicken Flan with Brown Rice Pastry	111
West Indian Chicken with Cashew Nut Butter	90

FISH

Cheesy Fish Cakes	64
Smoked Salmon Sausages	69
Smoked Salmon Tagliatelle with Red Pepper Sauce	52
Tuna Fish Casserole	141

VEGETARIAN

Green Bean & Cherry Tomato Stir-Fry	138
Leek & Potato Pie	76
Light Potato Rosti	86
Nutty Vegetarian Sausages	69
Peanut Roast	54
Swiss Cheese Fondue	75
Thai Vegetable Curry	141
Three Tomato & Feta Rigatoni	97
Vegetarian Kebbe	73
Vegetarian Lentil Lasagne	96

ACCOMPANIMENTS & SIDE DISHES

Celeriac Purée	101
Fluffy Spanish Potatoes	108
Glazed Potato, Turnip & Carrot Balls	107
Layered Salad	77
Light Potato Rosti	86
Luxury Potato Salad	108
Oriental Chicken & Cashew Nut Salad	97
Potato Purée with a hint of Garlic & Olive Oil	101
Sweet Potato Purée	102

SAUCES & DRESSINGS

Fresh Tomato Coulis	103
Mediterranean Tomato Sauce	52
Nineteenth Century Recipe for Salad Dressing	89
Olive Oil Mayonnaise	40
Onion Gravy	61
Orange Sauce	62
Pesto Sauce	92
Raspberry Coulis	103
Spicy Yoghurt Sauce	60

Buffet & Party Food

Beef & Black Pepper Sausages	70
Cajun Style Chicken Meat Balls	63
Cheese & Chilli Sticks	127
Cheese & Tomato Quiche	23
Chicken, Lemon & Chive Sausages	70
Chicken Tikka Kebabs	90
Chinese Chicken Sausages	68
Cool Crunchy Coleslaw	75
Curried Chicken Flan with Brown Rice Pastry	111
Fresh Orange Jelly	84
Grilled Millet & Parmesan Squares	114
Lamb, Rosemary & Lemon Sausages	67
Layered Salad	77
Luxury Potato Salad	108
Meat Kebbe	72
Oriental Chicken & Cashew Nut Salad	97
Pork, Fennel & Paprika Sausages	67
Soured Cream, Blue Cheese & Chive Dip	121
Vegetarian Kebbe	73

Desserts & Ice Creams

Almond Pavlova with Summer Fruits	43
Apple, Cinnamon & Yoghurt Ice	148
Banana, Orange & Lemon Sorbet	148
Banoffi & Ice Cream Pie	104
Basic Cream Recipe	120
Café Liégois (Instant Coffee Sorbet	56
Chocolate Caramel Bar Ice Cream	145
Chocolate Creole Ice Cream	146
Chocolate Pudding	111
Cream of Coconut Ice Cream	145
Creole Coconut Pie	85
Date & Buckwheat Pudding	114

Fresh Fruit with Crème Fouettée	122
Fresh Orange Jelly	84
Fudge Creole Ice Cream	146
Ice Cream Sprinkle	78
Indian Pistachio Nut Ice Cream	146
Individual Sherry Trifles	142
Lemon & Raspberry Posset	122
Macaroni with Raisins & Apricots	98
Mango & Lime Sorbet	148
Melon Balls in Juice	84
Mississippi Mud Pie	147
Potato Pancakes	134
Summer Fruits in a Raspberry Coulis	103
Vanilla Creole Ice Cream	146
White Chocolate Mousse	43

Cakes & Pastries

Almond & Apricot Roulade	133
Almond & Orange Sweet Pastry	24
Apple Strudel	78
Celebration Fruit Cake with Almond Paste & Snow Icing	16
Elevenses Cake	18
Hazelnut & White Chocolate Brownies	132
Luxury Mince Pies	24
Mini Brie Brioches	26
Oat, Honey & Apple Rock Cakes	113
Oat & Wholemeal Shortcrust Pastry	23
Open Fruit Tart with Almond Cream Filling	22
Passion Cake with Tangy Icing	44
Pithiviers (Rustic Almond Tart)	132
Puff Pastry	20
Rich Sweet Shortcrust Pastry	22
Scottish Potato Drop Scones	86
Scrumptious Chocolate Cake	15

Tarte Tatin	21
Vanilla Cream Cheesecake	19

Cookies & Biscuits

Almond Fudge Crumbles	131
Butterscotch Cookies	25
Cheese & Chilli Sticks	127
Chocolate Dreams	125
Grilled Millet & Parmesan Squares	114
Honey & Lemon Creams	126
Jamaican Crunchies	125
Kourambiethes	127
Mocha Triangles	128
Savoury Shortbread	25
Viennese Fingers	126
Walnut, Almond & Hazelnut Biscuits	131

Drinks

Banana Thickshake	56
Citrus Refresher	83
Exotic Fruit Cocktail	55
Fizzy Lemonade	83
Irish Coffee	118
Kenwood Lemonade	55
Mocha Fino	117
Morning Bright Eye	82
Pear & Pineapple Drop	82
Peppermint Coffee Crème	118
Summer Cooler	83
Tropical Spritzer	82
Turkish/Greek Coffee	117

Specialist Recipes

Avocado & Cucumber Face Pack	92
Banana & Yoghurt Baby Pudding	92
Home-made Butter	41
Lime & Lemon Marmalade	137
Orange & Lemon Curd	85
Orange Marmalade	138
Celebration Fruit Cake with Almond Paste & Snow Icing	16

INDEX

INDEX

Notes

NOTES

NOTES